How To Raise Good Kids

495

How To Raise Good Kids

Barbara Cook

BETHANY HOUSE PUBLISHERS
MINNEAPOLIS, MINNESOTA 55438
A Division of Bethany Fellowship, Inc.

Published by Bethany Fellowship, Inc.
6820 Auto Club Road, Minneapolis, Minnesota 55438

Printed in the United States of America

Cook, Barbara, 1939-
    How to raise good kids.

    1. Children—Management.   2. Children—Religious
life. I. Title.
HQ769.C67   649'.7   78-7844
ISBN 0-87123-233-2

TO MY MOTHER, HOLLY PAULSON

Whose devotion to mothering first inspired my quest for
excellence in the noblest feminine career.

THE AUTHOR

BARBARA COOK is the wife of Pastor Jerry Cook of the East Hill Church of Gresham, Oregon. She is the mother of three children as well as being a noted ladies conference speaker. Barbara is best known for creating "A Touch of Beauty," a women's ministry in the Pacific northwest which focuses on Bible teaching concerning homemaking, marriage, motherhood and feminine needs. From a single weekly Bible study she has developed a ministry extending far beyond the sphere of East Hill Church. The work now encompasses numerous Bible classes and a syndicated radio program which is carried in several states. There is also a monthly fellowship called "Kaffee Klatsch" attended by about 500 women who gather to share their faith and experiences.

Preface

A group of young mothers gathered in my living room to study the Bible as they would a college textbook. We wanted to know and to do God's will in raising our families. We'd heard the proposals of the experts for successful parenthood, and had become confused by the conflicting theories. We'd all vacillated between such patterns as parenting to please the neighbors and parenting to please the relatives. (Everything that moves and breathes seems to have advice for a young mother!)

I began to wonder, "What does *God* expect of me?" After all, in the end, it's to Him I'll answer for my mothering, not to the experts, or the relatives or neighbors. Did the Bible say anything specific about mothers besides "spare the rod and spoil the child"? In fact, was *that* even in the Bible? Or was it a Ben Franklin maxim!?

For a while I mentally suspended my preconceived ideas and knowledge accumulated in psych courses and magazine articles—even tried to shelve the philosophies of my capable mother and mother-in-law. I wanted to study the Scriptures with a totally open mind.

We asked questions like, "Why did God make children?" "When does punishment become child abuse?" "What causes rebellion?" "What do we do when children fight?" "How young can a child begin his relationship with Jesus?"

We found exciting answers to all the questions we asked. We found the Bible listed negative and positive rewards as the destiny of mothers, and that it gave direction in reaching the positive rewards. A concept of goal-oriented motherhood emerged in our minds.

The chapters of this book are mainly devoted to specific application of the scripture to a few goals under each of four primary responsibilities of mothers. Naturally, it is not comprehensive, since we have actually studied more than twice this many topics relating to motherhood—and are regularly taking up the study of new ones.

In 1972, through the encouragement of the women here at East Hill Church and that of my husband, we began sharing what we were learning by means of a daily radio broadcast, "A Touch of Beauty." These chapters were originally prepared as scripts for that program and also for the tape cassettes we provide for women's Bible study groups. It is our hope that putting into print what was formerly available only on tape will make it possible for these Bible studies to be more easily taught.

What I would like to see happen to women who read this book is a turning to Bible-oriented motherhood. If you study the scriptures we've listed on a topic and come to different conclusions than I came to, that's all right with me—the authority for parenting is not a writer or a psychologist or an educator, but the Creator of parents and children. I want to challenge mothers to think for themselves and habitually compare what they read and hear to God's opinions. Unfortunately, very few have enough knowledge of what God's opinions are on a given subject! Hopefully, this book can provide a starting point and a stimulus for that kind of honest searching. If I can get mothers to study the Bible as the textbook of their profession, I've succeeded!

Barbara Cook
Gresham, Oregon
1978

For information on Barbara Cook's cassette tapes or radio broadcasts, write:

A Touch of Beauty
P.O. Box 402
Gresham, OR 97030

Table of Contents

Section 1—Laying the Groundwork

Section 2—Training Your Child to Love and Serve God

Section 3—Training Your Child for Living

SECTION 1

Laying the Groundwork

Chapter 1

Is There Hope?

Have you ever found yourself thinking, "This is all beyond me!"? I'll never be able to raise good children in this crazy, mixed-up world. Is there any hope for me, a Christian mother, trying to guide my children in a society of relative morals and godless thinking? Dare I hope they will grow up to serve God? Or should I prepare for the worst, such as rebellion, drugs, running away and free love?

We were in a conference for Christian youth leaders. Over our coffee, two of us were discussing some of the alarming trends appearing on the horizon for today's high schoolers. As I remember, we were talking about Alvin Toffler's book, *Future Shock*; and this young leader said, very seriously, "My wife and I have decided not to have any children. Why bring them into a world like this, when we know the perils they face here? This planet is a frightening place!"

My reaction: "That's a very logical choice—if you happen to be a non-Christian, a parent who has no supernatural power in his home." However, this young husband was not an unbeliever. He was a Christian who was simply unaware that the Bible contains promises for parents living in this age—and not only promises but *specific instructions*.

In the Scripture, one of the titles for Jesus is "Wonderful Counselor." That's great news for parents. It means that I have a personal Counselor to advise me in this frightening challenge of motherhood. Because of this truth, and because the Holy Spirit is being poured out upon all flesh today, I don't feel negative about raising children during this time. In fact, I think it's the most exciting time in all history to be a mother! Let me tell you why.

You see, my children are in the Last Generation! We've had the Now Generation, the Pepsi Generation and the Peace Generation. Now it's the Last Generation. Jesus himself described these days, saying that when we see all these things coming upon the world, we are to look up because our redemption is drawing near. What causes fear in unbelievers brings joy to the mothers of God's kingdom. Never in history has there been an acceleration of fulfilled prophecy like this. Christians can see in the news reports the fulfillment of prophecy pointing to the end-time return of Christ for His Church.

Coupled with the anticipation of Christ's coming again is the glorious revival now sweeping the world. My children are growing up in the middle of this; their lives are being molded by it in a way that older generations have never known. My children are seeing God's power and beauty in the lives of young and old who really know Jesus. What a heritage! What an influence! True, they rub shoulders at school with spiritualism, séances, ouija boards, pornography and drugs. But in contrast to Satan's counterfeits, they're also seeing God's supernatural miracles. And *your* children are, too, if you have them in a church where the Lord is actively at work in lives. When our children live in an atmosphere of miracles, answers to prayer, and rejoicing, then we needn't have such small faith as to fear for their future!

The Power Is for Children, Too!

This great outpouring of the Holy Spirit that crosses the barriers of denomination, culture, and races is for our children, too, so that they will lack nothing in power or joy for these last days. That's what we're told in Acts 2:17: "And it shall come to pass in the last days, saith God, I will pour out of my Spirit upon all flesh: and *your sons* and *your daughters* shall prophesy, and *your young men* shall see visions, and your old men shall dream dreams."

A mother of seven first brought that promise to my attention. At one time in her life, Bobbi Wold worried about whether she could raise her children to serve God. The world they went into each day seemed so corrupt, so filled with temptations that it seemed hopeless to fight against the environment. As she prayed about her children, God directed her to read this passage. Bobbi claimed it as a promise for her little ones, and the Lord has been fulfilling it in the last few years, as one after another enters high school, and then college, faithfully serving Jesus with enthusiastic love. Do you want that for your children? Do you want the supernatural power of God flowing through their lives? Do you want your lovely teenage daughters prophesying, and your athletic boys seeing visions? It *is* happening, you know! It's happening all around us.

I've been with kids of all varieties in many parts of the country, as my husband ministers in camps and conferences—and they *are* prophesying. They're using all the gifts of the Spirit in a beautiful and sensitive way. Perhaps you're at home with small toddlers these days and have little contact with teens. So just to give you a glimpse into that world, let me describe my impressions of just one of these experiences, because it's nothing like what I knew as a Christian teenager.

One conference was at a resort in California. Three hundred high school and college kids from churches up and down the West Coast got together for three days of intensive Bible study and worship. These sons and daughters *did* prophesy! Some of those prophecies left an indelible impact on me. These were normal, fun-loving teens, full of good humor and intelligence, but intensely serious about the things of God. That place was so saturated with love—a love that *even included adults!* These young people had an insatiable appetite for the Word of God. They loved to hear it preached. They loved to discuss it, to sing it. There were kids from every kind of background— straight kids, hip kids, young teens and college students; white, black, Spanish, Indian, long hairs, short hairs, even a few adults with no hair at all!

No Parlor Games!

You can't help noticing that this generation of Christians is different from any of its predecessors. Christians of today are aware of the times in which they live; they're serious about the gospel and about reaching people for Jesus. They're done with games and phoniness; they're unmaterialistic, and turned off by materialistic attitudes. They're unimpressed by weak, powerless Christianity. They want the real thing, the kind of supernatural Jesus that Paul and Peter died for, not a Jesus Christ Superstar. And Christian teens enjoy Bible study—Bible study straight from the Scripture; practical, authoritative, the kind that doesn't cop out on intellectual questions. In get-togethers like this conference, I notice a spirit of rejoicing, of praising God, of freedom to express love, and freedom to be one's self in an atmosphere of celebration, punctuated by "Praise God"! "Hallelujah"! and "Isn't Jesus wonderful?"

In fact, to some adults, this kind of young person is just *too fanatical*! Committed, witnessing teenagers are a threat to their self-image, and it would be nice to write them off as irresponsible fanatics or as phonies. (After all, is it really necessary to go *that far* with this Jesus business?) Mother, if this feeling affects you, then for your children's sake, lay it aside, and allow yourself to be *inspired* instead. Quit *defending* yourself and begin dedicating yourself to God. Our adult generation has had such fear of fanaticism that kids have a hard time believing they love God at all!

This is the teen world my children are growing up into, and I'm glad! I hope they turn out to be some of the greatest fanatics for Jesus the world has seen! I'm encouraged when I see that they have a church full of terrific Christian young people to admire. What a blessing that they have an alternative to the hero worship of rock singers and movie stars.

Two Indispensables

I hope you're experiencing the same blessings with your children. If you want to raise kids who are committed Christians, then surround them with teenagers and adults who themselves are committed. Let them see the power and beauty of lives given completely to Jesus. Most important, BE A COMMITTED CHRISTIAN YOURSELF! That's the starting point, if you honestly want to be a successful mother in today's world.

In our congregation, when a baby is brought for dedication, the parents are first asked to dedicate *themselves* to the Lord. Then, as we pray together, the congregation is asked to dedicate themselves to so live the life of Jesus in front of that child that he will never have reason to turn away from God. We pray that the baby will learn from us what Jesus is really like, with no distortion, with no hurtful experiences at our hands. Both our *churches* and our homes are indispensable for successful motherhood.

Are You Serious?

This book is written for women who want to take motherhood seriously. I assume you wouldn't be reading it if that weren't your attitude. But in those moments when you're tempted to take motherhood lightly, discipline yourself with this verse, which describes Jesus' opinion of our influence upon a child: "Whoever receives one such child in my name receives me. But whosoever is an occasion for stumbling to one of these little ones who believe in me, it were better for him to have a millstone hung around his neck and to be sunk in the depth of the sea" (Matt. 18:5, 6).

Those are strong words. They show us how great is our responsibility to these fragile lives. Better to be drowned than to damage a child's response to Jesus. We need to remind ourselves that children are not cute little toys that are fun to cuddle and dress up. These little people are eternal souls, destined for a future that continues long after this life. So, if you want to have a fear as a mother, fear the judgment of God for your influence upon your child. That's a healthy fear, one you can do something about. Don't waste your energy fearing drugs or violence or society. The externals that surround our children can be neutralized by prayer and by claiming God's promises for protection. But a child's relationship to God—*we* have the influence to destroy that!

It's an awesome thing to realize that we will one day stand before God and answer the question, "What have you done with these children I've given you?" As a Christian mother, I'm sure you're working diligently toward the goal of 1 John 2:28: ". . . that, when he shall appear, we may have confidence, and not be ashamed before him at his coming."

And, of course, that brings up the question, "How can I tell if I'm doing the right things? I try to be a good mother. Will I succeed? So many have failed —how can I be sure I won't?" Well, that's where you must decide once and for all to whom you're responsible. If it's to God that I will account for my motherhood, then I must follow His directions for the project. If it's to my neighbors, or my family doctor, or mother-in-law, then I'll follow *their* directions.

Everybody has his plan for successful parenthood. The educators have their theories. The psychiatrists have theirs. Your relatives will propound their philosophies and you'll read those of the "experts" in *Woman's Day*. You can easily get confused—especially when these begin to contradict each other! So, settle once and for all whose directions you'll follow. In the final analysis, isn't the most logical belief that the One who invented children is the best authority? Why flit from one school of psychology to another, when they revise their theories every five years? Why look to astrology or sociology when God has written out for us complete instructions for motherhood?

That's the reason for this book—a group of young mothers gathered in my living room to study the Bible as they would a college textbook. We wanted to know and do God's will in raising our families. In countless Bible studies we've researched the Bible as one would study an encyclopedia, on every subject from discipline to children's friends. Some of what we've discovered is in these pages, and it's been tried and proved in actual Christian homes. We don't know all the Bible has to say on this, but we do want to share what we've found so far. The principles set down here are not based on sociological studies; they're not phrased to agree with any current fad in psychology. Neither are they based on my own experience as a mother. We need a better authority than subjective experience. I believe the best principles for shaping lives are the simple, direct statements of Scripture. If I should fail tomorrow as a mother, God's Word would still be true. If times change tomorrow, God's Word will still be true. In discovering His directions for raising children, we have the security of one stable authority, freedom from the contradictory voices around us, and we have confidence that we are following the leadership of the One who will reward us in the end. So begin now with me back where I began talking to God about my children. The first question I asked was, "Lord, what do *you* expect of me, a mother? I'm tired of worrying about other people's expectations. I want your opinions!"

Chapter 2

What Does God Expect
of a Mother?

Viewed next to the complicated concepts of child development experts, the Bible's requirements for a mother are refreshingly simple. It lists four responsibilities for us, and we'll see what they are in this chapter. But first, however, we need to ask an even more fundamental question: "Why did God make children?" Knowing the answer to that gives us the right perspective as we approach the four responsibilities. Another interesting subject of Scripture is the rewards of motherhood. We'll take up these questions in the following order: (1) Why did God make children?, (2) What rewards (negative and positive) does Scripture promise to mothers?, (3) What are the responsibilities God has given mothers?

Why Did God Make Children?

After all, He could have populated the earth with full-grown people in the same way He created Adam and Eve! Wouldn't it be a lot simpler than having people come into existence as wrinkled up, red-faced little creatures who insist on screaming and having their diapers changed? Many women feel that children are some sort of punishment, sent to keep them from enjoying life. They believe the arrival of babies has inhibited their life-style, kept them tied down, trapped. How many young mothers have you met that resent their children, merely tolerate them, or escape from them?

In the book of Psalms, we have a description of God's purpose in creating children: "Children are an heritage of the Lord: and the fruit of the womb is his *reward*" (Ps. 127:3). Now, a heritage is a gift, and a gift is usually appreciated. When your husband buys you a beautiful new dress for Christmas, puts it in elegant wrappings and presents it to you, how do you respond? Are you generally depressed, complaining, unhappy that he thought enough of you to give you something special? If that's your typical response, you probably don't receive many gifts!

When God presented you with that lovely newborn baby, He was honoring *you* in a special way, trying to give you something that would make you joyously happy. A gift is given to bring enjoyment and pleasure. It's received with appreciation and delight. We don't insult anyone, even a door-to-door salesman, by acting as though the gift is a nuisance, or by giving bored toleration. So, don't treat God this way! He gave you children to be enjoyed, to be a blessing and pleasure to your life. What a pity that many mothers don't realize this until it's too late! They spend the most precious years of life feeling sorry for themselves, wallowing in self-pity and resenting the babies that have stolen their freedom. Don't let it happen to you! Enjoy your children. Start today!

Degraded Motherhood

Attitudes that degrade motherhood are prevalent in America. That's because people are ignorant of God and His purposes, or worse yet, rebellious against Him. Consequently, we have a devaluation of human life; and a baby born is just another machine in a world of people who have been made machines, to be used and discarded. Without a personal, infinite God, human life loses all significance. After all, how can there be any meaning to *this* life if there is nothing beyond, and if we are not *persons*, individually designed by a loving God? That we are merely products of time and chance is the philosophical basis for legalized abortion and the trend toward infanticide. Historically, pagan societies have practiced infanticide because of this kind of humanistic, godless thinking. God is ignored, so *all* humans, and helpless babies especially, lose their value. How different when we know the One who said, "Children are a gift from God!"

What Rewards Does the Bible Offer Mothers?

Negative Rewards

As you study the book of Proverbs, you will notice a concept that I will state like this: "Motherhood is the most rewarding career in the world. But the rewards are *not necessarily good*! It all depends on our performance!" Just because I've brought a child into the world, changed diapers, and washed bottles doesn't mean I'll receive a great reward. Motherhood is probably one of the few jobs in the world where the pay comes only if the work is done right.

About once a year in my Bible study classes, I post a list of scriptures under the title, "Rewards of Motherhood." Beside each reference on the poster is a blank line (see page 32). As we read each verse together, we write on that line the rewards named. Making that list is both frightening and stimulating to mothers; it motivates us to do our best.

Here's the first verse on this list, Proverbs 10:1: "A wise son maketh a glad father: but a foolish son is the heaviness of his mother." The Living Bible puts it: "Happy is the man with a level-headed son: sad the mother of a rebel." Here we see two possibilities for a parent: *happiness* and *sadness*. Proverbs 15:20 suggests something else: "A wise son maketh a glad father: but a foolish man despiseth his mother." What a frightening possibility! No mother wants to be *despised by her own children*. We certainly don't want to work for this reward!

Proverbs 17:25 reads, "A foolish son is a *grief* to his father, and *bitterness* to her that bare him." Shame is another negative that a mother can experience. Proverbs 29:15: "The rod and reproof give wisdom: but a child left to himself bringeth his mother to shame." Have you had moments when you felt ashamed of your child? Like the time he threw a tantrum in the grocery store? Or the day he used his worst manners at your friends' house? Those small embarrassments are peanuts compared to the embarrassments we could experience from a *grown* son or daughter who never learns discipline.

Here's a quick summary of *negative rewards for mothers:* shame, sorrow, hatred, bitterness, grief.

Enough of that frightening subject! Now let's talk about the positive, pleasant rewards we can work for.

Positive Rewards

Proverbs 29:17 instructs, "Correct thy son, and he shall give thee rest; yea, he shall give delight unto thy soul." In modern English, that means, "Discipline your son and he will give you *happiness* and *peace of mind*." I like that, don't you? Isn't it amazing that in return for investing about twenty years in a child, you can receive an entire lifetime of happiness and peace? And I like this old English term, "delight unto thy soul." Thinking about that reward makes it a little easier to obey the part of this verse that says we must correct the child.

Proverbs 23:24-25 declares, "The father of the righteous shall greatly rejoice: and he that begetteth a wise child shall have *joy* of him. Thy father and thy mother shall be *glad*, and she that bare thee shall *rejoice*." I have a friend who fits this description perfectly. Julia Peterson and her husband have raised nine children in a wonderful Christian home. Every one of those children is a Christian, raising his own family to serve God. Counting grandchildren, the family now numbers over fifty, and these fifty continually shower Julia with love and blessings.

Many years ago, the inspired writer put down, "There is a generation that curseth their father, and doth not bless their mother" (Prov. 30:11). That's a good description of the kind of world we live in today; it's true that we're seeing a lot of kids totally lacking in respect for their parents. But there's another kind of generation also making an appearance, growing up right alongside these. It was illustrated to me one night in a service. A beautiful teenage girl stood to testify. She said, "I'd like to thank the Lord for my wonderful Christian parents." I noticed that tears of joy came to her parents' eyes. Then tears began to flow down her cheeks as she finished, "My parents," she said, "have taught me more about Jesus and helped me more with my spiritual life than anyone in the world." Now *that*, Mother, is what the Bible is talking about when it describes a good mother in Proverbs 31, and promises this tremendous reward: "Her children arise up and call her blessed!" May it happen in your lifetime!

What Are the Responsibilities God Has Given Mothers?

According to the Bible, God's expectations of us are simple and clear. Once we've decided that it's to Him we're responsible, we can relax and enjoy motherhood. These splendid rewards we've been looking at are given by God to mothers who accomplish the task well. But He's not so mysterious as to hold out a lovely reward and then keep us in the dark about the way to gain it! He defines in the Bible the specific things a mother is to do for her child. Then He gives detailed instructions on the ways we can accomplish these things. There are four basic things that God asks of us mothers. We could call them "The Bible's four commands for mothers," or, "God's instructions for raising children."

The first responsibility is quite obvious, at least to American women. (It's not necessarily taken for granted in *every* part of the world, though!) It's found in 1 Timothy 5:8, which states that you must PROVIDE FOR THE PHYSICAL NEEDS OF THE CHILD. "If someone does not take care of his relatives, especially the members of his own family, he has denied the faith and is worse than an unbeliever." This includes feeding the child, clothing him, keeping him clean and healthy, seeing that he gets proper rest, diet and exercise. Such things as innoculations, dental checkups, and putting bandaids on cuts are the mundane things the Bible is talking about here. An up-to-date child-care book will give you the details on this, and will help you know what to expect at each age in physical development. If all these unglamorous items strike you as trifles a governess or baby-sitter could handle, then look at it this way: You've been chosen to baby-sit for God! The child is really His creation and His possession. You're the governess He has commissioned to be stewardess of a life! That's an honor! It's also a little heavy. He goes so far as to say that if you're neglecting the physical needs of your family, don't bother to call yourself a Christian!

All of us have heard stories about women who are too "spiritual" to take care of their families—the ones who overbalance themselves with prayer meetings, Bible studies, Ladies Aid meetings and church potlucks. Children are left alone at home while Mom "serves the Lord." Their clothes are neglected, meals are hit or miss, and they run the streets unsupervised. Tragic accidents happen to such children. These children all suffer to one degree or another if a mother is deluded about her "calling."

Many American mothers are conscientious in this area. But they tend to forget that it's not the *only* duty of mothers. If you're providing for the physical needs of your child, you're actually doing one-fourth of what God asks. There's more!

God's first commandment to mothers: PROVIDE FOR THE PHYSICAL NEEDS OF YOUR CHILD. But the second, found in Titus 2:4, is: LEARN TO LOVE YOUR CHILD. "That they [the older women] may teach the young women to be sober, to love their husbands, to love their children, to be discreet, chaste, keepers at home, good, obedient to their own husbands, that the word of God be not blasphemed." This passage, by the way, is a fundamental description of the role of a wife and mother, with many implications. God understands the need of children for a mother's love. He made them with that need. But evidently He also realizes that we need to be *taught how* to love them. In one sense, love is a learning experience.

You see, love is not emotion. It's not just affection. (Although you *will* surely show affection to a child, demonstrating love in a way he can feel.) Love seeks the best for its object, regardless of the emotions of the moment. In the years of life with your children, your emotions will run the gamut from lethargy to strong affection. You'll experience anger, frustration, tiredness, disgust, delight, pride, embarrassment. It's important to remember that these feelings are neither the essence of love nor the absence of love. Love is never described in the Bible as a feeling. It's defined as a pattern of behavior toward a person. Even when you *feel* angry, you can do what's best for the ultimate good of the child.

Read 1 Corinthians 13 to see exactly how that works out at a practical level. Love does not relate selfishly to a child, seeking only what pleasure you can get out of him. Love does not destroy a child as a person, by treating him with rudeness and harshness. Love will consistently be asking, at each stage of growth, "What are the needs of this child at this point in his life? What will most help him to be the happy and whole person God had in mind when He sent him into the world?" The ways you love a two-year-old are different from the ways you love a teenager. That's why it's important to have the attitude, "I'm *always learning* how to love my child."

In all this talk of love as action—a non-emotional commodity—I'm not seeking to underrate displayed affection—cuddling, hugging and kissing. Those things are very important, too. Use lots of them! We need affection, whether we're adults or children.

During the thirties, many parents followed the popular psychological theory that babies should be raised stoically. Emotion was bad. "Emotional" was a very insulting word, used by this school of thought to describe affectionate parents, evangelical churches, and insane persons. A mother of that generation, whom I will call Martha, shared with me one day her personal suffering: "We didn't pick up a baby; we let him cry. We restrained ourselves from cuddling and hugging, even when we felt like it; it was *for the children's good.*" Today she has two grown children who are unable to enjoy life—or people. Marriage is a struggle for each and, worst of all, for Martha—they can't love *her*! She's damaged the one relationship that would be most valuable in her old age!

If you're serious about this second commandment for mothers, then the third will also be your desire: TEACH HIM TO KNOW AND SERVE GOD. Many scriptures state this commandment, probably the best known being Ephesians 6:4: "And, ye fathers, provoke not your children to wrath: but bring them up in the nurture and admonition of the Lord." It mentions "fathers" specifically, but I'm sure you agree this is the joint responsibility of both parents. That is implied elsewhere in Scripture. What is the "nurture" of the Lord? Well, have you ever nurtured a small plant? It needs to be surrounded with an environment of warmth, moisture, and food. So, our children need to be surrounded with an environment made up of the warmth of God's love, the moisture of the Holy Spirit, and the food of the Word of God. This beautiful word "nurture" also implies that a child *feels* surrounded by the tender love of his heavenly Father.

The verses my children have memorized in Sunday school have continually emphasized this attitude. The first verse Carmen ever learned, at twenty-four months of age—just barely able to talk—was, "We love him because he first loved us." And, of course, like typical proud parents, we asked, "*Who* first loved us?" Immediately the answer was, "Jesus!"

It's important to know that the nurture and admonition of the Lord is not "cramming religion down his throat," or a boring daily session of doctrinal instruction. A child is best trained to love and serve God in an atmosphere of loving example, in a setting of happiness and comfort. Imagine the impression made on children who daily hear the Word of God read and explained by parents who show in voice and attitude that they believe and respect it.

Let's go on to look at this word "admonition." It's necessary, too, and it refers to the *teaching* that takes place in this "nurture" environment. Admonition is verbal instruction, formal or informal. It includes teaching a child both the beautiful, positive promises of the Bible *and* the negative, frightening warnings. The environment won't do the job without the information; and the information won't do the job without the environment. One of the two is missing in a home where you hear, "My parents *forced* their religion on me."

What I really want for my children is nothing less than the warm and loving relationship with Jesus that I've found. I can't be satisfied if they only know *about* God. They must grow up knowing Him personally, as the Saviour, Baptizer in the Holy Spirit, Healer, and returning King. I'm aware the choice for salvation is ultimately in the hands of each individual, but at least we can prepare children in such a way that when they are confronted as adults with a personal commitment to Christ, they will understand it, they will *want* it, and they can follow through to live as mature and productive Christians.

How young is a child able to receive Jesus as his Saviour? How soon can he really understand? Well, why not encourage every response a child makes to Jesus, at every age? Much depends upon the home he's in, the amount of teaching he has, the capacity to think and listen; but the Holy Spirit knows how to communicate with children, and He deals with them at various points of life, asking for a commitment of their lives at each age. And as a child matures, he knows increasingly the demands of that commitment. Our girls had reached the ripe old ages of twelve and ten when we were amused to hear them counting up the years they had been serving the Lord. "Mom, I've been saved eight years!" said Carmen. "And I've been a Christian seven years," chimed in her little sister. Granted, they haven't been saved *"out of"* much sin! But they certainly have been saved *"from"* a life of sin! When I first knelt with each one, and at her request, led her to accept Christ as her personal Saviour, I had a few doubts. But today each can recall with perfect accuracy the time and place of her commitment, including the events leading up to it. And Jesus takes a child seriously. That child can never be the same again. Even his periods of rebellion will be nagged with the uncomfortable awareness that Jesus loves him and pleads with him.

What a privilege and what a joy that God has given us in this commandment! Teach your child to love God. Teach him to know Him personally, and serve Him because of His love.

Now the fourth responsibility follows on the heels of that. It's possible for a child to grow up loving God but trained to be a failure in life. He has a miserable time trying to live for God because he lacks certain basic necessities like the ability to get along with people, the discipline to work and earn a living, or even the motivation to get out of bed in the morning. What is lacking? TRAINING FOR SUCCESSFUL LIVING. This responsibility is spelled out in Proverbs 22:6: "Train up a child in the way he should go: and when he is old, he will not depart from it." (Incidentally, while he's young, he *may* depart, but just be patient and watch him return to his training when he's mature—say, 25-35.) Notice it doesn't say, "*Tell* a child the way he should go"; it's "*Train up* a child...." It's possible to be telling a child one thing and at the same time be *training* him something very contradictory.

This principle is a law of cause and effect. It's like the "reap-what-you-sow" law that God has written into the universe. This verse is a commandment, but it's also a statement of the way things are. For a Christian parent, it can be a wonderful promise. But for a godless parent, it's a frightening threat. Training a child is done in every home in five ways, for better or for worse! These are actually five things we all do continually. They mold a child's habits, attitudes and life. And it's *how* we use them that determines *what* we train. I call them:

1. Example
2. Encouragement
3. Explanation
4. Experience
5. Emendation (correction)

Example: Examine your own home, and see if those aren't the things influencing each child. Ask yourself,

"What am I training by my example and the examples of people who come and go in our home?"

Encouragement: What things am I *encouraging*, and what things am I failing to encourage by praise and appreciation? For instance, a child who gets a lot of attention when he's naughty, but not very much when he's good, is being *encouraged* to misbehave. A little girl who's excessively pampered when she's sick is being encouraged to be sickly. A child who is commended for the neat papers he brings home from school is being encouraged to do neat work.

Explanation: The way you explain things to a child, or fail to explain, is powerful. For example, a child asks, "Where do babies come from?" To give no answer is one kind of explanation. It communicates ideas that will form a child's view of himself, ideas less accurate than you'd want him to have! Your explanations of why we go to church, why we share the toys with little brother, who God is, why not to run into the street—you make them daily, sometimes in an exasperated frame of mind, because kids ask *so many* questions! Watch your explanations carefully. Think them through and put them in words a child can understand. And, remember, silence *is* an explanation! Sometimes it's a wise explanation, and sometimes it's a dangerous one.

Experience: What about experiences your children are having? What are they learning from them? Are they learning that there are consequences to breaking rules? That life has dangers as well as pleasures? Are they learning confidence or fear? Are they learning how to handle disappointment? We can't control all the experiences our children have, but we *can* control a *majority* of the *life-shaping experiences.* And we can view each new experience as a teaching time, and pray for guidance about using it to teach the things we really want learned.

One day our five-year-old came in crying with a broken heart. A girl down the street had yelled at her, right in front of everyone, "I don't like you, and I don't want to play with you!" What could she learn from an experience like that? Inferiority, withdrawal, fear? After a little comforting, I tried to minimize the importance of it by saying, "No matter how nice you are, there will always be *some* people who don't like you. That's all right, because you have lots of friends who *do* like you. You have Robin, and Chris, and Carolyn, and Jill and. . . ." That's a valuable truth to learn—that *everyone* isn't always going to like me. Some adults are miserable because they've never learned that! So, if Carmen could learn it in a relatively minor, though painful incident, the experience was used to her benefit.

Emendation: We called correction "emendation" to follow the other four E's. A large number of mothers rely on correction alone as a means of training their child. They don't realize it's only one of five tools God has given. And they are unaware that they're teaching just as much by example, encouragement, explanations, and experience as they are in the punishments they dole out. Consequently, the five don't work toward common goals, but work against each other. Virginia had a thirteen-year-old son who kept getting caught smoking at school. Every time this happened, Virginia's husband administered a hard spanking with his belt. As it continued, they added to the punishment "being grounded" for a week at a time. All this seemed to do no good, and Virginia would report to me her desperation to get that boy under control. I could hardly suppress my dismayed laughter: as she and her husband would discuss the next punishment for Tom, they invariable finished off a pack of Marlboros!

On the other hand, a Christian mother recently related this story: Her thirteen-year-old son found a pack of cigarettes on the way to school. He decided to become instantly popular by sharing them with his friends; by noon he found himself suspended from school, along with his sick friends. When Jeannie came home around 1 o'clock, she found her sobbing teenager lying on the floor, with the suspension letter in his hand. Soon his father came home from work, took off his belt, and administered the same discipline Virginia's husband had. Then his son was made to work off his days of suspension by doing all the housework for a week, the laundry, bed making, dishes and cleaning. Result: He never smoked again—or broke *any* school rules! With this boy, *correction* was effective, because his parents' *example* showed smoking was undesirable, their *encouragement* was "don't smoke," their *explanations* were convincing, and his *experience* was such that the smell and taste of tobacco was not a familiar, natural thing that was made easy to accept by living in an environment where it existed.

Correction, of course, isn't always physical. With some youngsters, one word gets action. Simply stating, in a calm voice, "No, don't touch that," is correction. You don't have to be unpleasant to correct, or angry or vindictive. Correction isn't always punishment, although we shall see that the Bible views some amount of punishment inevitable in the course of training a child. Depriving a child of privileges is correction; so is being made to sit still on a chair for fifteen minutes—or playing alone in his room because he's quarreling with the other children. "Rebuke" and "reproof" are two terms the Bible uses for correction. While a Christian mother shouldn't get into the habit of yelling, nagging, harping and screaming, we'll admit that reprimanding *is* one of our duties, and, without it, we'll have children who don't really understand what their limits are.

So, those are the tools we work with: example, encouragement, explanation, experience, and correction. Now, we need to ask, "What are we going to do with the tools? What are the goals of our training?" Even an animal trainer has certain goals; he knows when he's succeeding and when he's not. So, let's look now into the Bible for suggestions of goals appropriate for a Christian mother. I know you don't want to carry out your career in a hit-and-miss way, having only a fuzzy notion of what you're working for. You want to use your tools in a purposeful, intelligent way, to raise a child who can love and serve God, and who can live successfully on this earth.

Have Your Own Bible Study

What Does God Expect of a Mother?

1. Why did God create children? Psalms 127:3

Ge 1:28 God created male, female, & said, Be fruitful & multiply, & fill the earth & subdue it, & rule over the fish, & birds & over every thing that moves.

2. What rewards does the Bible offer mothers?

Negative	*Positive*
Sorrow (Prov. 10:1)	Delight unto thy soul (Prov. 29:17)
Hatred (Prov. 15:20)	Happiness (Prov. 29:17)
Grief (Prov. 17:25)	Peace of mind (Prov. 29:17)
Bitterness (Prov. 17:25)	Rejoicing, joy, gladness (Prov. 23:24, 25)
Shame (Prov. 29:15)	Grateful, affec-
Cursing, ungrateful offspring (Prov. 30:11)	tionate children (Prov. 31:28)

3. What are the responsibilities God has given mothers?
   (a) Provide for the physical needs of your child (1 Tim. 5:8)
   (b) Learn to love your child (Titus 2:4)
   (c) Teach your child to know and serve God (Eph. 6:4)
   (d) Train your child for successful living (Prov. 22:6)

Five tools to use in forming good habits and attitudes in your child: example, encouragement, explanations, experience, and emendation (correction).

Chapter 3

What Are Your Goals?

Here's an old cliché, very trite: "To fail to plan is to plan to fail." We've heard it many times, and we accept the concept it expresses in business management, in household management, in money matters, even vacation trips. But when it comes to raising children, we never seem to get quite that organized! We don't know what we want for them, so consequently we'll never know whether we're succeeding or failing in the commandment to "train up a child." Success in any venture means you have a predetermined goal and are moving toward it.

God has entrusted parents with a life that He created for a definite purpose. *How much* of the fulfillment of that purpose depends upon them? Larry Christenson says that each child comes into the world with a set of sealed orders, a unique destiny. It's the parents' job to help the child discover that destiny and to so prepare him for life that he won't be stifled by hang-ups. So much potential is within a child, placed there by the Lord—creative talent, artistic abilities, intellectual capacity, physical prowess. None of us fully develops all his potential. But what a tragedy it is when almost *none* of what God has visualized in a child is discovered because parents are so blinded or so insensitive that a child's greatest abilities never have a chance to come forth.

God's Art Work

God's plans for your child may not include the unfulfilled ambitions you once had. We can't assume that children are carbon copies of their father or mother. Psalm 139 gives us a glimpse into the individual art work God performs each time a woman experiences pregnancy. I use it as a basis for answering a child who asks, "Where did I come from?" or "How come I have freckles?" One verse in this chapter says, "Thine eyes did see my substance, yet being unperfect; and in thy book all my members were written, which in continuance were fashioned, when as yet there was none of them" (v. 16). This is a description of an embryo, a child in the very first days after conception. The word translated "substance," which is "yet being unperfect," in Hebrew is the word *golem*—a wrapped up and unformed mass. But this passage tells us even at that point, God sees the complete work of art. The Master Designer has His architectural drawings all made out. "In thy book all my members were written" —my legs and arms, the size of my bones, facial features, the color of my eyes and skin. In fact, Matthew 10 states that even the hairs on my head are numbered! We can accurately and confidently tell a small child, "God has a wonderful plan for your life. He made you special for a special work. No one else is exactly like you and no one else can do exactly what He's put you here to do."

A child who knows *that* about his creation will never doubt his worth or the love of God for him as an individual. And when a mother knows that about her child, she becomes very conscious of her stewardship in his destiny.

With this stewardship in mind, one Wednesday morning in a Bible study we decided to search the Scriptures for goals the Lord would recommend. We made a big chart, listing the qualities we found. On one side of the chart the title read, "What God wants for my child." We drew a line down the middle and on the other side the title read, "Therefore, I will not allow." For every positive character trait the Bible encourages, there's the contrasting negative trait which it discourages. The two opposites cannot coexist. For example, the first positive trait we listed was *obedience*, based on Ephesians 6, which says, "Children, obey your parents in the Lord, for this is right." Therefore, we cannot allow disobedience. <u>True obedience is prompt, willing, and cheerful</u>. Therefore, I must <u>discipline *myself*</u> to <u>correct the grumbling, arguing</u> kind of compliance that children often fall into.

Ways and Means

If we pursue obedience as a goal for a child, what does that mean? Let's look at our five tools again. First, we mothers <u>set the *example* of obedience and respect</u> to those <u>God has put in authority</u>: our pastors, civil authorities (yes, even the patrolman who gives you a speeding ticket!). We consistently <u>*encourage* obedience with appreciation</u> for the things children do for us. ("Thank you, Tim, for doing such a good job cleaning the kitchen tonight." Or, "I'm so glad I have a wonderful girl like you for a daughter.") We see to it that the child's *experiences* of obedience far outweigh the experiences of disobedience, so that a habit pattern is set. We *explain* (but not *too* often), the scriptures that teach obedience. We must make sure our children know the Word of God on the subject so that they're aware it's right not because Mom and Dad are stronger than they but because *God* said it is right! And of course, we must *emend* disobedience when it appears. It can't be ignored and it can't be allowed to go on.

Another goal that appeared on our list as we studied obedience was <u>respect for authority</u>. The negatives that cannot exist with respect are many, such as a smart mouth, a scornful look, back talk, rudeness, sullenness and a rebellious attitude. These would be the things we <u>correct</u>, while <u>at the same time commending</u> courteous behavior, exemplifying it, <u>explaining rules</u> of courtesy toward other people. <u>Example is the key</u> here. If I want <u>my children to treat me with respect and honor, they must see me treat Daddy that way</u>. Melva Koch has often mentioned how impressed she was as a girl that each evening around 5 o'clock her mother made a point of having her set the table and get everything <u>looking ready for dinner</u>, "Because," her mother would say, <u>*"Daddy* might be home at any minute now."</u>

This gave Melva a feeling that Daddy was a very important person, more honorable than even the mayor or the president. And it keyed her whole relationship with her father. No matter how strict his rules seemed at times, she respected him too highly to ever defy them.

Here are some other goals that were added to our list: honesty, confidence, motivation, vitality, diligence (the ability to work hard cheerfully), ability to get along with people, love for others, self-control, unselfishness, kindness, wisdom, patience, happiness, purity, knowledge, courage, joyfulness, and dependability.

We didn't include specific spiritual qualities in this list because those came to our attention in another study, about training a child for relationship with God. We called that one "Habits and Attitudes for Healthy Christians," and you'll read about it farther on. This list is made up of basic character traits that the Bible talks about, in terms of what I called earlier, "training for successful living." You'll find it interesting to do your own study on this and make your own list of goals.

Let's take a closer look at this list, still thinking of our five tools. If you want *self-control,* for example, what are the negatives you must correct? Well, you can't allow a child to give in to unrestrained anger, temper tantrums, and prolonged self-pity spells. *Patience* means we correct impatience, sharpness. (An area for concern here, too, is a child's impatience with himself.) What about diligence? We have to provide the experience of hard work and accomplishment. We can't allow laziness, which in our generation seems to be a nonchalant, unenthusiastic pattern of living which revolves around the TV set.

A scripture in Ephesians 4:32 motivated us to put the trait of *kindness* on the list. "And be ye kind one to another, tenderhearted, forgiving one another, even as God for Christ's sake hath forgiven you." The most effective *explaining* can well be to read that verse with a child and help him memorize it. Most Sunday schools have the first part, "Be ye kind," as one of the first lesson texts for two-year-olds. We *encourage* acts of kindness to others, perhaps suggesting he color a special picture for Grandma or take a popsicle out to the neighbor boy. Remembering that we're to encourage kindness will be helpful in that dilemma you feel when your toddler wants to give away a toy to his friend. We encourage kindness when we notice and praise thoughtful acts a child initiates on his own. We also let him see *examples* of courtesy and kindness in the home. And we let him *experience our kindness when he cuts a finger, or needs help in finding a lost toy.*

Kindness is the basis for all systems of etiquette, and that's why we teach manners—little things like saying "please" and "thank you," and manifesting the attitude "you first, me second." What an insult to teach kindness, practice flawless courtesy to your adult friends, then turn on your child with scathing rudeness when he irritates you! I confess I've been guilty of this. And the Lord has quickly rebuked me!

Innoculate Against Fear

Now let's talk about *courage.* A good verse for *explaining* is also one that Sunday schools use for toddlers: "Be not afraid, for the Lord thy God is with thee" (Josh. 1:8). The negative alternative to courage is fear, so we must deal with children's fears in a sensible and understanding way. To build courage, we must *encourage* new experiences, new ventures that will develop confidence.

Our second grader came home from school one day asking what a talent show was. After I'd explained, she decided she wanted to enter and play a piano solo! Well, to put it mildly, her mother had a few fears at the thought of her competing with seventh and eighth graders! I could imagine an embarrassing experience for all of us. The temptation to *dis*courage was very strong. But then I remembered the multitudes of talent contests I had entered as a child and teenager—undoubtedly I *had* made a fool of myself in some of them. But just stepping out into the unknown had certainly built my own courage and confidence. And, you know, that's exactly what happened to Carmen. She experienced the sense of accomplishment that comes from doing something scary like playing the piano in front of five hundred people. That one experience so built her confidence that she was ready to try all kinds of new things. (And even though *I* played "Fiddler on the Roof" every night in my sleep for two weeks of silent fear, *she* breezed through it like a professional!)

Is Happiness Your Habit?

Happiness is another goal we mentioned on our list of positives. Do you know that happiness is a habit, and a habit we can build into a child just as readily as the habit of brushing teeth or making a bed? Contrary to the popular opinion that happiness is something to be *pursued* (giving the impression that it is somehow elusive and circumstantial), happiness is an attitude that comes by personal choice. To help our children make the right choice, we have to correct and refuse to allow whining, complaining, arguing and resentment. And we have to refuse these things in our own lives too. Eric Fromm claims that today's children need happy mothers as desperately as they need loving mothers. Lots of loving mothers make miserable persons out of their offspring simply because they refuse to be happy people themselves. And how can a child experience happiness without living in a home where it predominates?

Jesus' Childhood

Now let's look from another angle at this matter of goals for children. Let's look at the childhood of Jesus. Luke 2:40 puts it in capsule form: "And the child grew, and waxed strong in spirit, filled with wisdom; and the grace of God was upon him." Then Luke 2:52 adds this about adolescence: "Jesus increased in wisdom and stature, and in favor with God and man." That really stands out to me because it's precisely what I want to say about my children in those years between twelve and twenty: that they're growing in wisdom as they're growing in height and weight; that they're developing in their relationship with God and they're learning to have good relationships with people. This just about covers the four areas of life:

physical growth, mental growth, social growth and spiritual growth. A teenager who's seeing a well-rounded maturing in these four areas is headed for a good life.

Balanced Growth

At the time I was first thinking about these things, I could look right out my window and observe some encouraging samples of balanced growth. I was teaching in Crestview's Junior High Camp. Christian kids were growing up all around me, including many from my own church. It seemed like only yesterday that Pam was a second grader in the Sunday school. Now she was nearly up with her dad in stature! She was going into eighth grade, and coming along nicely with growth in wisdom, stature, favor with God and man—awkward and fumbling at times, but moving in the right directions. Looking out my window, I saw her come out of the chapel. She'd been in there praying with several others, developing in her relationship with God. Then she sauntered up to a group of girls and entered the conversation, probably about boys! But she *is* growing socially. Her mental growth was noticeable when she stood in my class and read a scripture passage with real understanding.

Incidentally, the experience of being in a Spirit-filled, well-managed Christian camp once a year is invaluable to a child. No Christian family should deprive children of this opportunity. If money is a problem, *pray* for the registration fee. Or take a part-time job for a while to get it! It won't replace a good home church, but it *can* do things no church setting can accomplish.

Jesus Was No Weirdo!

What we really want to see is wholeness—completeness—in our children—so that they become well-balanced adults, able to move with ease and confidence. None of us wants to raise a misfit or an oddball. We don't want for a child the misery that comes from lopsided development in any one area to the neglect of other areas. And Jesus is the pattern for a well-adjusted personality. He was a perfectly balanced person—loving God but also able to relate well to people. He grew tall and strong. He had a healthy, disciplined body. But He also had a trained mind, free from the distress that comes from ignorance or lack of education. When we look at Jesus, we see the kind of personality God wants for our children. He was liked and respected as a teenager and as a young man. Even later, when religious leaders turned against Him, it was not because of an obnoxious personality. Therefore, I see that God wants for my child a wholesome social growth. And I will encourage those activities that will bring social development. Friendships, group outings, the church and the school are the natural places for this to happen. And I don't believe that taking a Christian stand at school means my child will be thought of as "some weirdo." Jesus was well-liked as a teenager, and *at the same time* growing in God's favor.

Growth in wisdom is important, too, and a trained mind is valuable to God. School *is* important, and grades give some indication of progress. Make it a point to know your children's teachers. Keep in touch with them about the mental growth of each child; you'll find you can solve school problems while they're *small* problems and avert the big ones. Take an interest in the papers they bring home, even first-grade coloring sheets. And pay attention to the report cards. Look into the excuses given for a bad grade. Check it out.

The Final Touch

But there's something more that took place in Jesus' life and it's also a pattern for wholeness in our children. He was popular, respected, spiritual, brilliant, healthy —everything you could ask for. But we don't read of Jesus, the very Son of God, performing one mighty act before this event. In all His perfection, He had to be filled with the Holy Spirit before His supernatural ministry could begin. Remember reading how the Spirit came upon Him at His baptism in Jordan? John the Baptist saw Him descend in the form of a dove. Jesus went out to defeat Satan in the wilderness *in the power of the Holy Spirit,* then returned to make this announcement in His home church: "The Spirit of the Lord is upon me, because he hath anointed me to preach the gospel to the poor; he hath sent me to heal the broken-hearted, to preach deliverance to the captives..." (Luke 4:18).

Jesus did no mighty works until He had become the *anointed* Messiah. A perfect personality will not bring forth a supernatural ministry. And no matter how brilliant my child may become, how talented, how popular, he still needs to be filled with the Holy Spirit. And I want to be alert to this as he is growing up—not to push him into it, but to provide the opportunities and teaching, a Spirit-filled youth group, youth Bible studies, rallies and camps.

Last summer one of my friends sent her rebellious daughter to Camp Crestview. Kay didn't even want to go, but while she was there, the Lord dealt with her and one night she walked forward, asked to be saved and filled with the Holy Spirit. Kay's rebellion ended that night, so completely that after a few days at home, her unbelieving father could no longer restrain his curiosity. "*What* has happened to that girl?" he demanded. As his wife explained, he ordered, "Send the rest of our kids to that camp!"

The filling with the Holy Spirit is not an emotional experience a child has once and then forgets; it's a way of life, a source of power that puts excitement into Christian living. It's the doorway into realizing all the potential God placed within you for His kingdom. Today's teens are becoming powerful New Testament Christians. Spirit-filled teens in our church pray for the sick and see them healed. They are used in prophecy, the word of wisdom and the word of knowledge. They see miracles happen through their own ministries, and the supernatural becomes natural. Living any other way would be so drab and boring, who would want to do it?

If *Jesus* needed the power of the Holy Spirit, *my* children need the power of the Holy Spirit!

Have Your Own Bible Study

What Are Your Goals?

What God Wants for My Child: (positive goals in character building)	*Therefore, I Will Not Allow:* (negative opposites)
1. Obedience (Eph. 6:1)	Disobedience
2. Respect for authority (Eph. 6:2)	Rebellious attitude, smart mouth, back talk, scornful look, rudeness
3. Self-control (Prov. 14:29; 16:32; 25:25)	Unrestrained anger, temper tantrums, prolonged self-pity spells
4. Patience (1 Thess. 5:14)	Impatience, sharpness
5. Diligence (Prov. 15:19; Rom. 12:11) (Enthusiasm, motivation and the ability to work)	Laziness or nonchalant disinterest
6. Kindness (Eph. 4:32)	Rudeness and selfishness
7. Courage and confidence (Josh. 1:9; 2 Tim. 1:7)	Fear and timidity
8. Happiness and joy (1 Pet. 3:10; Phil. 2:14; 4:4) (love for life)	Depression and complaining
9. Love for others (Rom. 12:10; James 4:11; Titus 3:2)	Criticism
10. Ability to get along with people (Matt. 5:9; Rom. 12:18; Eph. 4:31; Prov. 17:14)	Quarreling
11. Honesty (Rom. 12:17; Eph. 4:25 & 28; Prov. 11:1)	Lying, cheating, stealing
12. Wisdom and knowledge (Prov. 2:4-9; 8:33)	Ignorance and lack of education
13. Purity (2 Tim. 2:22)	Perverted thinking or wrong information about sex
14. Friendliness (Prov. 18:24; 2 Tim. 1:7)	Shyness
15. Dependability, loyalty (Prov. 11:13; 25:19) (Responsibility and faithfulness)	Irresponsibility

Balanced Growth:

Luke 2:40 and Luke 2:52:
Spiritual development
Physical development
Mental development
Social development

waxed- increase in vigor, be strengthened

stature - maturity in yrs. or size, age

The Final Touch:

Luke 3:21 and 22:
Luke 4: esp. 1, 14, 18:
Being filled with the Holy Spirit

Chapter 4

Correction: What Does the Bible Say?

Before we go into specific ways of training a child, let's get a clear picture of what the Bible does and doesn't say about correction. Although it's not the only tool we work with, it is an important one, or there wouldn't be so many scripture passages about it.

Any mother can study the Bible for herself on this subject. Just take the book of Proverbs, read through it, and mark every verse you come to that talks about correcting children. After reading them *all* (not just one or two), write down the conclusions you come to. That's what we've done here, but there are many verses we haven't space to include.

The Nature of Children: Good or Evil?

A startling verse for the 20th century is Proverbs 22:15: "*Foolishness* is bound up in the heart of a child; but the rod of discipline shall remove it far from him" (NAS). Now, if that's God's opinion of the nature of children, what do you think He would say to parents who raise families on a philosophy of self-expression? This theory rests on the false assumption that man is basically good. Therefore, if a child is just allowed to grow up "naturally," without getting inhibiting correction from his parents, he will develop as nature intended. He will automatically make the right choices, automatically express good things. If you really believe this, then to be consistent you should allow the child to eat whatever appeals to him, because he will choose the food his body needs (mud pies, lollipops, ice cream!).

Don't dictate when to rest and when to play because, after all, when he needs it he will *want* to rest.

According to the Bible, man is *not* basically good, not even a child. When any child expresses himself without restraints or guidance, he expresses his sinful nature. He brings forth not only those things that will develop him into a mature person but also those things that will destroy him.

Proverbs 29:15 states, "The rod and reproof give wisdom: but a child left to himself bringeth his mother to shame" (KJV). What does that show about the extremes of lawlessness we've seen in the sixties and seventies? Could there be a correlation between a generation of parents afraid to correct and a generation of teens expressing open rebellion?

Correction Is Not an Option

"Correct thy son, and he shall give thee rest; yea, he shall give delight unto thy soul" (Prov. 29:17). That's a command, not a suggestion! If we obey the command, we can expect the promise for delight.

Here's another interesting verse: *"Chasten thy son while there is hope,* and let not thy soul spare for his crying" (Prov. 19:18). The old English word "chasten" means "to spank with the intention of teaching and training." You're not really chastening a child when you lash out at him in anger, or, like the old woman who lived in a shoe, merely spanking because you don't know what else to do! Chastening is purposeful and discriminate. The child understands exactly what it is he's being punished for. Mother has explained *what* he has done wrong and *why* it is wrong. He knows it's because he's loved that he's being corrected, not just because she feels angry with him.

"Chastening while there is hope"—that's for those of us with very young children. We must do it before their habits are sealed for life. There will be a time when we're too late. It's better for Junior to cry now than for us to cry later—over our failure!

Correction Has Eternal Results

This concept is found in Proverbs 23:13, 14: "Withhold not correction from the child: for if thou beatest him with the rod, he shall not die. Thou shalt beat him with the rod, and shalt deliver his soul from hell.'' We are affecting a child's eternal destiny if we withhold discipline from his life. A child who does not learn that there are always consequences for disobedience will have a difficult time living as an adult who can obey God. How many adults do you know who live immature, floundering Christian lives because they cannot discipline themselves? Jesus said that any man wanting to be His disciple must deny himself, take up his cross and follow Him. The Christian life demands discipline, and one of the best ways we can prepare a child to live for Christ is to have a home where discipline is consistent, strict, and fair.

In these days so close to the return of Christ, we *must* produce children who can live committed, consistent Christian lives. Those Christians who are floundering just now are not exactly enthusiastic about the Rapture. They're fearful! There is really something to this principle of correcting your child to deliver his soul from hell!

The rod is mentioned so often in connection with discipline that I tend to feel God agrees with the people who say you should never use your hand to spank a child. It's safer, both physically and psychologically, to use a stick. I don't know what you visualize when you hear the word "rod," but I used to imagine a long, cruel piece of metal! Actually, it was just a spanking stick—perhaps a willow branch. In our house, it would be a ping-pong paddle; maybe in yours, it's a big wooden spoon.

The Hebrew word for rod in Scripture literally means "a stick, twig or branch from a tree." A child "shall not die" or be physically damaged if a rod is used, says Scripture. But parents who violently lash out with their hands or grab the nearest belt buckle are in no sense fulfilling this Bible directive—and there are children who have died tragically!

Correction Is Not Child Beating

One Sunday my husband preached a sermon on this

subject, and a young man became irate with him. He was normally a well-controlled member of our congregation, but on this Sunday he approached Jerry ready for battle. Brian was a social worker in a boys' detention home. He felt that nearly all the boys in trouble were the product of cruel parents. They described their homes as places where harsh fathers and step-fathers beat them for every small misdemeanor. Brian misunderstood the biblical approach to discipline because he had seen it perverted.

That's one reason it's important to see that at the same time the Bible commands correction, it also warns that Christian correction is never unreasonable, selfish, or uncontrolled. It cannot be an expression of anger; it is an expression of love—often the most difficult expression of love. Look again at Ephesians 6: *"Provoke not your children to wrath:* but bring them up in the nurture and admonition of the Lord." This same concept is repeated in Colossians 3:21, "Provoke not your children to anger, lest they be discouraged." The Greek word translated "discouraged" is *athumeo,* meaning to "have the spirit broken." God warns us to watch that we do not become severe, cruel, or harsh. In fact, the passage we quoted earlier in this chapter about chastening your son while there is still hope seems to also carry a warning about child abuse. Both the Berkeley and the Resived Standard versions state this verse, "Discipline your son while there is hope; do not set your heart on his destruction" (Prov. 19:18). Another translation has it, "Do not desire his death" (NAS). The Amplified Bible says, "Discipline your son while there is hope, but do not [indulge your angry resentments by undue chastisements and] set yourself to his ruin." The Septuagint translates it, "Chasten thy son, for so he shall be hopeful; *and be not exalted in thy soul to haughtiness."* I think there is a strong insight here into the delicate balance of our parental emotions. We can easily cross the line into rage while correcting a child. In *great humility* we need to be always conscious of our need for God's wisdom and self-control. Nothing is more tragic to me than parents who practice child abuse and rationalize it by their misguided notions of scripture. These people face the judgment of God for offending—damaging—the little ones who believe in Him. Child-beaters are held responsible by God for punishment, even if the courts fail to penalize them. Cruel parents do raise bad children—children whose spirits have been so broken, they've given up trying. That's what Brian had seen—kids who had been disciplined without love, told they were no good and never would be; now they were living out the unlovely picture projected for them.

One good rule of thumb is to never punish a child when you *feel* angry. Send him to his room. Get control of your emotions; then explain to the child why he's being punished. Let him know always that any form of correction you use is because you love him, not because he's irritated you or because you think he's no good.

Correction Is Security

In our early years of marriage, my husband and I spent our time working with teenagers. Kids in trouble would confess their transgressions and in tears mourn, "My mom didn't even punish me! She didn't care!" We'd hear teens begging us to tell them they couldn't do certain questionable things. When Jerry would set down a firm "No! It's wrong and you can't do it!" they were delighted. At last they had an inkling of the security that comes only from firm boundaries. Hoping their parents would give some direction, the kids would ask *them* the same question. But the parents would hedge, fearing rebellion. Even recently, Becky sat in Jerry's office and cried, "I know I should be mature enough by sixteen to make these decisions for myself. But I'm really not, and it would help so much if Mom would just say NO! Left to myself, I'm terribly afraid of what I'll do."

I remember the day when I learned this lesson for my own family. Carmen was two and having a very naughty day. Busy with housework, I didn't stop to correct her. As the day went on, she became outrageously uncooperative! I finally dropped everything and went after the paddle. I walked over to her and said, "Carmen, do you want a spanking?" In a very serious voice, she answered, "Wes, Mommy."

How practical the Bible is when it says, "He that spareth his rod hateth his son, but he that loveth him chasteneth him" (Prov. 13:24). And Proverbs 3:11, "My son, despise not the chastening of the Lord; neither be weary of his correction; for whom the Lord loveth he correcteth; even as a father the son in whom he delighteth." This verse is quoted and interpreted in Hebrews 12:7, 8: "If you endure chastening, God dealeth with you as with sons; for what son is he whom the father chasteneth not? But if ye be without chastisement, whereof all are partakers, then are ye bastards, and not sons." The whole point being made is that love is expressed in correction and only a parent who doesn't care will neglect it. We can understand God's loving correction only because we have experienced the same type of love and security from earthly parents. (By the way, the definition we gave earlier for "chastisement" still applies when you talk about the chastening of the Lord. It's not some mysterious sickness, given for an unknown reason that we'll "understand better by and by"; it's purposeful, discriminate, and dealt out for training and teaching when *we* disobey.) The Christian knows exactly why he's being chastised and how to correct his behavior. The book of Jonah is a good example of this. Personally, I prefer to learn my lessons from the warnings and commands in Scripture, so that my Father will seldom need to chastise me! One of our children has that same attitude toward her father; she's smart enough to straighten herself out with just a word from him; consequently she rarely gets any "chastising."

One question mothers often ask is, "How hard should I spank?" Well, a spanking should be an event, not a little swat. It should be an experience that is painful and not commonplace. The effectiveness is lost if you use it for every little misdemeanor. *Do* stop far short of child beating, and *do* use the place on the body God created for discipline. Never slap a child in the face or hit his back, arms or legs. Four or five good swats with a paddle is sufficient. When I was teaching seventh graders, we sent unruly boys to the principal for such "counseling." I've seen some tough big boys come back crying pathetically after five such swats! (Whether the pain was to the body or to the pride, they didn't say.)

Surprisingly, some of the most precious times I've had as a mother have come in the time following a spanking. When the child stops crying, I always go in and love him awhile and we talk about the kind of person he will be when he grows up. Sometimes we have prayer about the problem at hand. It's in these times I understand the beautiful verses in Proverbs 23:15: "My son, if thine heart be wise, my heart shall rejoice, even mine. Yea, my reins shall rejoice, when thy lips speak right things."

It's an event in our house when Daddy gives a spanking. That's reserved for things that need the impetus of final authority. One of these "events" turned into something wonderful. A negative trend had developed: our nine-year-old was gaining almost too much confidence, becoming arrogant and willful quite often—no outright disobedience, just the beginning of a rebellious spirit. Little "dirty looks," smart answers—that type of thing. Daddy decided it had better end before it really became a problem. He and his daughter spent time behind closed doors. There was a discussion, followed by the unmistakable sound of the paddle. Then crying, followed by tender loving, and a repentant prayer. The poor girl, left to herself, sobbed like her heart was broken (it was—she had disappointed her father), then she fell asleep. When she awoke, there was a changed expression on her face. Her eyes looked different; she was prettier than she had been for weeks. Her restlessness disappeared along with her quarrelsomeness and complaining; she began to obey sweetly with no attitude of rebellion. Her father's correction had made her heart to be wise and her lips to speak right things. And now we enjoy what the Lord promised: "My heart shall rejoice, even mine. Yea, my reins shall rejoice!"

Have Your Own Bible Study

What Does the Bible Say About Correcting
Your Child?

1. The nature of children: Prov. 22:15; 29:15.
2. Correction is not an option: Prov. 29:17; 19:18.
3. Correction has eternal results: Prov. 23:13, 14.
4. Godly correction is not child abuse; punishment is not to be unreasonable, cruel, or uncontrolled—not an expression of a parent's anger: Eph. 6:1-4; Col. 3:21; Prov. 19:18.
5. We express love in correcting our child and giving him security: Heb. 12:6-8; Prov. 3:11; 13:24; 23:15.

Chapter 5

Rebellion: Causes and Cures

Remember the verse we mentioned in Chapter 4 about the nature of children; that foolishness is bound up in the heart of a child and the rod of discipline will remove it from him? Not only is rebellion an abominable thing in God's sight, it's also something you can count on. If your child is rebellious, congratulations! You now have proof he's really part of the human race! The Bible doesn't even qualify its statement by saying "foolishness is bound up in the heart of *some* children"! Face it, we've all been rebellious, ever since Eve rebelled against God in the garden. She insisted on doing her own thing and so did Adam. Since then, each of us has had this inherent stubbornness, this unwillingness to submit to authority, even the authority of God. If you have a rebellious child, it's not necessarily because you're too strict, or haven't let him express himself enough. Even if you're a perfect parent, your child will find it natural to rebel. He'll need that rod of correction. But to deal with rebellion in your child, you must first deal with it in yourself. (Remember the powerful tool of *example!*)

Are You a Rebel?

So, how about your life, Mother? Are you proud of your rebellion against your parents? Still rationalizing about playing that adolescent game? Do you boast about your rebellion against the Church, your family, or society? The issue isn't whether *they're* right or wrong; the issue is *your attitude.* A rebellious attitude will keep you from the blessings of God, no matter what you're rebelling against. Perhaps it is rooted in resentments toward your husband and his leadership, or against God and His plans for your life. You'd rather do it yourself, for better or for worse—even though you know it'll turn out for worse! Many women are rebelling against their role as homemakers and mothers; they're dropping out, or fighting "the establishment." Whatever form it takes, rebellion is the same old sin that Lucifer began when he challenged God and took a third of the angels with him. You can say you're "crusading" against the government, the law, or "standing up to" the pastor of your church; but if you have real courage, you'll face rebellion for exactly what it is: SIN AGAINST GOD. Handle the rebellion in your life every time you handle it in your child; that practice will keep the resentments cleansed from you before they grow into big, thorny hang-ups.

You see, without this critical tool of example, all your explaining will be empty words, and your correction will have to be done over and over again, with no apparent results. A child can sense when you have a stubborn, rebellious spirit; subconsciously he will accept that spirit as admirable, because it's part of his beloved mommy.

Only one expression of rebellion is encouraged in the Bible: rebellion against the devil and his kingdom. Hate him and destroy his work wherever you see it. But let your relationship with God and your husband be one of loving respect. Renounce your rebellion; confess it in prayer to the Lord, ask His cleansing, and then begin to walk in obedience. Do it for the sake of your children!

Prayerful Prevention

Now, that same pattern can be used in dealing with a child's rebellion. It must be confronted with the Word of God, renounced, repented of, and cleansed. Rebellion is not the kind of thing you deal with once and for all. Thoughts and attitudes sneak in that build up to rebellion, and a mother must be watchful so that she can strike the ugly head when it first begins to rise, *not* after it has gone so far as to have its fangs entrenched!

Someone asked Susannah Wesley, undoubtedly one of the greatest mothers of history, her opinion of the most important principle in raising children. She had raised ten to become godly Christians. She wrote a short essay, answering that the secret was to bring the child's will into submission. With each child, she worked consistently to train immediate obedience by the age of two. Her concept was that the stubborn self-will had to be conquered and kept under control, and that if this self-will were allowed to prevail, it would take a child straight to hell. It's that spirit of "No one's going to tell *me* what to do" that *must* be brought into subjection by the parents if the child is ever going to learn subjection to God. This may sound harsh, but the same grown children who described Mrs. Wesley's strictness also related memories of her tenderness and warmth toward them.

Ruling the stubborn will of a child does not mean breaking his spirit, making him into a scared rabbit. It's teaching him respect for others. You see, rebellion is the opposite of obedience. Rebellion is present when a child talks back, argues, or looks at you with an insolent sneer. Obedience is not truly obedience if it is not instant and respectful. "Delayed obedience is disobedience," my mother used to say. When you tell a child to pick up his clothes and he waits five minutes to begin, that's the time to insist on obedience. Teach him that you expect him to do exactly *what* you ask and *when* you ask it, *not* when he feels like it. Children are great procrastinators and excuse-makers. If you want to be a conscientious mother, start by handling these small infractions and you'll prevent rebellion before it ever becomes a problem. It's so much easier to enforce your authority when the resistance is only delay and excuses than when the resistance is out-and-out hostility. So no matter what ages your children are, insist on prompt obedience. Don't put up with grumbling, arguing, talking back or pouting. If Susie is asked to clear the table after dinner, make sure she does it respectfully and cheerfully.

Scripture Speaks

If it gets further than this, however, and a child

continues in a bad attitude, take him to the Scriptures. Whether it's rebellion in terms of his speech or in the friends he's choosing, confront him with the scripture on that particular subject. After a time like this, when you see a change for the better, remember to comment to your child. To illustrate: A child was developing the habit of agruing. In private, I said something to this effect: "Honey, I've noticed a bad habit in you lately; it's arguing. I want you to read some verses to me. Then I think you'll want to ask Jesus to help you talk right." I had her read aloud verses like, "A fool's mouth enters into contention and his lips call for strokes," "Hatred stirreth up strifes; but love covers all sins," "Leave off contention before it be meddled with." (For small children, we usually read these in a modern version.) Before long, she understood that arguing was wrong, not because Mommy said so, but because *God* said so. She willingly prayed to renounce it and asked for help in using her mouth right.

You Can Control!

You see, it's *not* impossible to control rebellion! It's not something you have to stand by helplessly and watch. I realize many parents have fallen into the trap of hopelessness and defeat, but that's *not* the teaching of the Bible. Christian parents needn't be sucked into the mold of this world, but many of them are, to the destruction of their offspring. The responses of typical parents to rebellion are just pathetic! They fear it, ignore it, rationalize it, yell and scream at it, and wring their hands while deploring, "We don't know what to make of him!" (One response—"How about a nice rug?")

Fear Manipulates Parents

In some homes, parents have *feared* rebellion so much, they've done away with rules, thinking it's simpler to just let a teenager do what he wants than to have rules he may rebel against. The ultimate in rebellion—that of running away from home—is such a horrible fear that a smart teen can use it to wheedle almost anything out of his folks. (By the way, the story of the prodigal son in Luke 15 contains a wealth of wise advice for parents whose children leave home in rebellion, and this wealth is lifted out beautifully by Dr. James Dobson in his book, *Dare to Discipline*. He points out that the father didn't beg the boy to stay home, didn't cry or throw a temper tantrum, but let him go. Then the father was wise enough to sit back and wait while the boy experienced the consequences of his rebellion. He didn't bail him out of the difficulties his rebellion got him into; he just waited until the money ran out, the pig sty grew uncomfortable and the son "came to himself." This, of course, was an adult rebel who had chosen a dropout life-style on his father's bank account, but there are some principles in it that apply to any parent with a child who's into extremes of rebellion. One of these indispensable rules is that of forcing the rebel to face the music every time his rebellion runs him aground. If he steals a car, he'll have to stand trial; Daddy won't bribe the judge. If he gets kicked out of school, Mom won't take the principal to task; she'll see that he pays the penalty and learns that life out of school is even tougher than life *in* school.

Fear is one dangerous response to rebellion; another is to cop out, to give up. This kind of mother stands wringing her hands with despair: "I've lost him; it's too late now, he's beyond my control. I did my best, now he has to decide for himself; he won't listen to me!" This mother believes that rebellion is the end of hope, that it's uncontrollable and incurable.

The Father Who Failed

Perhaps that's the way Eli felt. Do you remember Eli, in the Old Testament, the priest who trained Samuel? He was a man of God, dedicated and holy. But Eli brought the wrath of God down upon himself and his family when he failed to stop the rebellion of his sons. Listen to these frightening words in 1 Samuel 3:13: "I am about to punish Eli's house forever, for the iniquity which he knew, because his sons were blaspheming God and he did not restrain them." Eli mourned, he agonized, but he did not have the courage to stand up to a couple of smart alecks and put an end to their rebellion. More than once the Lord warned him, but Eli's tears never turned into action. Meanwhile, his grown sons spread their corruption throughout Israel; they were dishonest public officials, pilfering priests, stealing in the temple from the Lord himself. They were swingers, living in sexual sin and encouraging others to join them. Finally the Lord had had it; in one day He wiped out Hophni, Phinehas, and their procrastinating father, Eli.

What Are We Really Saying?

It is just as tragic today when Satan deceives moms and dads to the point where a loud-mouthed kid can back them up against a wall. Rebellion is a sin and God holds you responsible if you allow a child to continue it. What we're really saying when we declare, "I just can't do a thing with him," is that we can't do it without giving up time, or pleasure, or whatever it takes to follow through. "I can't do anything *without* giving up my popularity and getting him mad at me." Do you love your child enough to risk his wrath, to do what's best for him even if he seems to hate you for it? Do you love him enough to interrupt your work or your telephone conversation to enforce a rule?

Law enforcement agencies are saying it's the laziness of parents that's to blame for juvenile delinquency. Rebels are on the increase not because parents have been too strict but because they've feared strictness and become pushovers. Here's a summary of rules drawn up by the police department in Houston, Texas. It is called:

Twelve Rules for Raising Delinquent Children

1. Begin with infancy to give the child everything he wants. In this way he will grow up to believe the world owes him a living.
2. When he picks up bad words, laugh at him. This will make him think he's cute. It will also en-

courage him to pick up "cuter" phrases that will blow off the top of your head later.

3. Never give him any spiritual training. Wait till he is 21 and then let him "decide for himself."
4. Avoid use of the word "wrong." It may develop a guilt complex. This will condition him to believe later, when he is arrested for stealing a car, that society is against him and he is being persecuted.
5. Pick up everything he leaves lying around—books, shoes, and clothing. Do everything for him so he will be experienced in throwing all responsibility onto others.
6. Let him read any printed matter he can get his hands on. Be careful that the silverware and drinking glasses are sterilized, but let his mind feast on garbage.
7. Quarrel frequently in the presence of your child. In this way he will not be too shocked when the home is broken up later.
8. Give a child all the spending money he wants. Never let him earn his own. Why should he have things as tough as *you* had them?
9. Satisfy his every craving for food, drink and comfort. See that every sensual desire is gratified. Denial of his desires may lead to harmful frustration.
10. Take his part against neighbors, teachers, and policemen. They are all prejudiced against your child.
11. When he gets into real trouble, apologize for yourself by saying, "I never could do anything with him."
12. Prepare for a life of grief.

God preserve us from the insecurity that demands our kids understand and like us. Deliver us from playing popularity games with them. Those things are so temporary when you remember that a grown-up "foolish son [rebel] *despises* his mother" (Prov. 15:20). While raising this foolish son, you may be popular with him; it's *later on* he hates you because you had neither the strength nor love to stop his folly.

Parents Pass the Buck

Now if all that doesn't convince you to be a mean, old-fashioned strict mother, get a copy of David Wilkerson's book *Parents on Trial*, written from the backdrop of those grisly stories you've read in *The Cross and the Switchblade*. Wilkerson went to the parents of criminals, drug addicts and gangsters, hoping to discover the flaws in homes that would produce such failures. Do you know that *every parent* refused to accept responsibility? One father said, "I taught Bobby what was right and what was wrong; he just rebelled against me, that's all. He wouldn't listen." Another said, "It was his friends—he's in prison today, because his friends led him into a life of crime." All the parents of hardened criminals claimed they had done their duty; not one would admit he'd made a mistake! So David Wilkerson talked to the kids. "What could your parents have done to keep you from messing your life up like this?" Over and over, the kids' answer was that the parents' big mistake was in *allowing* rebellion. "If my mom had loved me, she would have *stopped* me from running around with those wild kids. Instead, she just nagged me about it and went on with her housework." (Sounds remotely like Eli, doesn't it? Her talk never turned into action, just like Eli's tears never turned into action.) Another boy was deeply hurt when his parents didn't love him enough to punish him when he began rebelling. "They just gave up," he said; "that's how much they cared." Following one heartbreaking story after another like this, *Parents on Trial* makes a strong case for dealing with rebellion at every age—including high school. The softness of parents trying to avoid rebellion has only encouraged it. In fearing the results of being too strict, they've handed the kids responsibility too heavy for them. That's why that teenage girl sat in my husband's study begging him to tell her "no." Her parents had forced decisions on her beyond her spiritual maturity. She *knew* what was right but didn't have the moral fibre yet to *do* it. While *she* left the study feeling relief because someone had disciplined her, her *parents* sat home agonizing over her rebellion, wondering what they could possibly do with her. Like many, they were limping along with threats, nagging, and angry arguments, using action only as a last resort when pleading and reason had failed.

Learn from the mistakes of others; rebellion is a sin. Rebellion will destroy all God's plans for the life of your child. When your child rebels, God holds *you* responsible to stop it. Don't cop out!

Chapter 6

Take Out a Real Life Insurance Policy

Wouldn't it be wonderful if you could take out an insurance policy on your child's happiness—just pay monthly premiums and rest assured that everything good would come to him? If there were such a policy, you'd be sure to invest in it, wouldn't you? Think of the time and money you're now investing in your child's future: those dental bills, those property taxes for schools, the medical checkups, to say nothing of extras like swimming lessons, clubs and the orthodontist.

Parents *do* put time and money into the things they're convinced have value. But few of us invest heavily in the single most valuable product of all. This overlooked commodity *is actually* a life insurance policy for a child's happiness. The coverage is so complete, so wonderful, most people just can't believe it. But, perhaps, after reading the next few pages, *you'll* believe it. And if you do, it will determine your priorities for investment of time, money and effort.

The thing I've been talking about here is a *knowledge of the Word of God*. If what it says about itself is true, then teaching it to a child is of more lasting value than a good education, a musical skill, a flawless smile, or an Olympic medal. To parents who invest in it, the Bible offers overwhelming promises.

You see, God's Word is powerful, and it is enduring. It will outlive you and your authority over a child. Plant the Scriptures in his heart and they will stay there through a college education or a stint in the army. Philosophies will come and go; he'll *not* be snared, if the truth is in his mind ahead of them. The Word of God will remain in his heart long after he's forgotten everything the music teacher taught. It will remain no matter how deep into sin he tries to go. Adults who have returned to Christ after straying have recounted how the scriptures they'd learned would haunt them in bars, how the Word would hound them, make them sick of the life they were leading and remind them of the joys they were missing. Once a child has a knowledge of the Word, he has a basis for living the rest of his life. God has promised, "Heaven and earth may pass away, but my word shall *never* pass away."

Brains in the Bible

Consider now the relationship between the Bible and a child's mental, intellectual development. The Bible is the only book in the world that promises its readers more than knowledge of a subject. It offers all the things needed for knowledge to work: wisdom, understanding, intelligence and the ability to make correct decisions. Those are the very things parents spend thousands of dollars on by the time a child reaches twenty-one.

Education That Sticks

But alas! we still have universities capable of turning out a well-educated fool! Haven't you seen instances of the kind of Ph.D. who ruins his life for lack of common sense? So listen, parent, to the opening words of the book of Proverbs:

> The proverbs of Solomon, the son of David, king of Israel; to know wisdom and instruction; to perceive the words of understanding; to receive the instruction of wisdom, justice, and judgment, and equity; to give subtilty to the simple, to the young man knowledge and discretion (Prov. 1:1-4).

These claims are made not only for the book of Proverbs; in that book and the Psalms, they're made for all the laws, precepts and words of God. In this one section, you will notice four mental qualities: (1)

knowledge, (2) wisdom (common sense—using the
knowledge you have in practical, everyday life), (3)
understanding, or comprehension of the things around
you—the world and people and events, (4) intelligence
("subtility to the simple")—literally that means making
a stupid person smart! The Living Bible puts it:
"I want to make the simple minded wise!" Here's hope
if you happen to have a child who is mentally slow
or has a low verbal intelligence score. For a youngster
who has reading difficulties, begin feeding him a daily
diet of Scripture as you would a doctor's prescription
of vitamin supplement, and watch his capacities grow.
Don't sit by passively and blame God for cheating Johnny
when He handed out the brains! God has declared
His will for your child very clearly in His Word: total
wholeness—mentally, spiritually, emotionally and
physically. We can overcome a mental handicap by
believing prayer and the power of the Word of God.
We will *not* overcome it with labels of "dumb" and
"stupid," or by pushing him faster than he's able to
go in school.

Gary had grown up with a severe reading disability.
As an adult, he could not read a book and understand
it. After committing his life to Christ, he began reading
his Bible and found he *could* understand that, so he
read, and read, and read! One Sunday, he shared something
with me that was just beautiful. The Lord had
given him a vision: a simple picture of a cross lying
flat on a hillside. Gary watched as the cross slowly
rose from the ground until it stood upright. It was then
he noticed that written across it were three words,
"A New Mind." He was still wondering what to make
of it, when the next day Gary felt a strong desire to
read a book. He picked up David Wilkerson's *The Cross
and the Switchblade*, and for the first time read a book
with delight and understanding. I wish you could have
shared the joy I felt that day, as I realized God was
doing a miracle right inside a grown man's head! The
Psalmist knew about this kind of power resident in
the Scriptures. He wrote: "The entrance of thy words
giveth light; it giveth understanding *to the simple*"
(Ps. 119:130).

Emotional Togetherness

Now, consider the Word of God and the emotional development of your child. Emotionally disturbed children are becoming alarmingly commonplace. Certainly no parent has planned it that way. We want emotional health for our children; not fear, anxiety, or turbulence. Here's a promise about that:

> My son, forget not my law; but let thine heart keep my commandments: for length of days, and long life, and *peace*, shall they add to thee (Prov. 3:1, 2).

Or Psalm 119:165:

> Great *peace* have they which love thy law: and nothing shall offend [upset] them.

In these days of mixed-up teenagers, wouldn't you just love to have a peaceful one! It's not really too much to ask for. If the stabilizing influence of the Bible is heavy in his life, a teenager can escape the turmoil we seem to accept as part of growing up. He can actually be a peaceful person who gets along with the family; he can avoid that whole stage of inner restlessness and tension. Peace is probably the most essential quality to emotional health, and a child at any age can have it if he's given the Word as conscientiously as he's given his daily nutrients. This means he has freedom from fear, confusion, and the majority of misery-producing emotions.

Another element of healthy emotional life is a positive attitude—a cheerful, optimistic outlook. The Bible calls that "hope," and promises it to those who know God's Word:

> Remember the *word* unto thy servant, *upon which* thou hast caused me to hope. This is my comfort in my affliction: for thy word hath quickened me (Ps. 119:49, 50).

Children raised without the Word have no knowledge on which to base hope; despair is a logical philosophy for them. But where there is knowledge of the eternal future our Father has planned, there is hope; there's reason for a cheerful attitude. The Scriptures make the difference between a negative child and a positive child. Two other emotional qualities are mentioned in this passage: *comfort* and *quickening*. We can comfort a child just so long without babying him; there is a point when he'll no longer allow us to take him in our arms and kiss away the tears. Imagine doing that for your sixteen-year-old who just failed to make the football team! But in that instance, his Father will comfort him very well, and without damaging his masculinity— *if* he's established the habit of reading the Word.

"Quickening" is an old English word for enthusiasm or motivation. It involves mental alertness, keenness, a will to live, and a zest for life. Children, like we mothers, have "down days"—they need a fresh shot of adrenalin now and then. In fact, there are some who seem to have *no* enthusiasm—for anything! A positive pattern of emotional development involves enthusiasm for life, an eagerness to learn, to do new things, to explore and be active. In Psalm 119 the concept of quickening (or motivation, enthusiasm) is continually tied to the Scriptures. For example "Quicken thou me according to thy word" (v. 25). "Quicken me after thy lovingkindness; so shall I keep the *testimony of thy mouth*" (v. 88). "I will never forget *thy precepts*: for *with them thou hast* quickened me" (v. 93). "I am afflicted very much: quicken me, O Lord, according to thy word" (v. 107). Do you begin to see why people who are enthusiastic about the Word are also enthusiastic about life? Giving a child that Word will give him a constant supply of motivation and eagerness for school and play—maybe even for getting out of bed in the morning!

I Wanna Be Free

How easily the free spirit of a child can be shackled! Instead of an uninhibited, expressive personality, we often see emerge in adolescence a cramped, bound up and fearful one. The varieties of emotional hang-ups are endless: fear, abnormal shyness, despondency, nervousness, feelings of inferiority and insecurity. Freedom from these plagues is as valuable to your child as freedom from polio and diphtheria. And this is what the Bible says about it:

> I will keep thy law continually, for ever and ever; and *I will walk at liberty*, for I have sought thy precepts (Ps. 119:44, 45, RSV).

What could be a better definition for freedom from hang-ups than "walking at liberty"! The Scriptures are designed to have a liberating effect upon your child. And, Mom, if emotional hang-ups have hemmed *you* in, they can liberate you too!

So far we've looked at the Word of God in relation to the mental and emotional development of a child. But now let's look into some verses that deal with his physical development. Recall what we read earlier of Jesus as an adolescent who "increased in wisdom and *stature*, and in favour with God and man." Let's look at the promises that connect the Word of God to physical development and also social development.

The Key to Long Life: Vitamin W

Modern life insurance policies are wonderful. But they don't really insure *life*—only money to your survivors when *you lose it*! However, the Bible *does* offer to insure life, if you'll pay the premiums. Please consider these verses:

> My son, attend to my words; incline thine ear unto my sayings. Let them not depart from thine eyes; keep them in the midst of thine heart. For they are *life* unto those that find them, and *health to all their flesh*. [note: health to their *flesh*—not to their soul only!] (Prov. 4:20-22).
>
> My son, forget not my law; but let thine heart keep my commandments: for *length of days*, and *long life*, and peace, shall they add to thee (Prov. 3:1, 2).

Is that life insurance, or is that *life insurance*?

You can protect your child from ill health and premature death. The mortality rate among teenagers raises yearly, but it needn't affect Christian families. Teens are losing their lives to suicide, drugs, murder and traffic accidents. In all these, there's an obvious correlation with the breakdown of obedience. A child who learns the Scripture will know rebellion cuts life short. In addition, he will learn the promises for healing and health, safety and protection. Those promises may save his life! If you pay the premium for your child, consistently giving him the Word, he will be the beneficiary in the most secure life insurance policy there is.

Popularity and Peer Groups

Perhaps this sounds like an unspiritual statement to you: I want my children to be popular. By that I mean that I want them to experience the respect of their peers, having learned to relate acceptably at a social level. Having friends and being well liked *does* matter! It's not a selfish lust; it's a vital part of growing up.

Mr. and Mrs. Winters had a seven-year-old boy named Sean. They were proud of his "Christian stand" at school. Whenever we visited in their home, Sean would tell of his latest "persecution" from the Godless children in his class. What the Winters didn't perceive was that Sean's problem was not his "Christian stand" but his inability to relate to other children. This boy knew how to talk in pious terms and amaze adults, but his social growth with his own age group had been neglected. Years passed and Sean attended a Christian college, a *spiritual* Christian college; sadly alone, he was still unable to make friends in his peer group! He could no longer blame it on persecution!

Jesus grew in favor with God *and with man.* The Old Testament was the parental encyclopedia of Jesus' day, and it has this to say about popularity:

My son, forget not my law; but let thine heart keep my commandments:

Let not mercy and truth forsake thee: bind them about thy neck; write them upon the table of thine heart: *so* shalt thou find *favour* and good understanding in the sight of God *and man* (Prov. 3:1, 3).

Do you see it? Learning the Word of God, making it a part of your subconscious thinking, is a key to adequacy in social growth. In our own group here at East Hill Church, we have many young people who prove it, in high schools and on college campuses. They're kids who spend time in the Word; they sing it to guitars; they spend their spare evenings at Bible studies, and their college lunch hours in prayer meetings. These are not the local misfits; they are respected, well-known students, who carry a powerful influence in their world.

That's the kind of popularity I'm interested in, the kind that stems from a natural self-confidence and friendliness, not the kind that comes from being squeezed into the peer-group mold. The popularity parents fear is peer-group pressure causing Christian kids to compromise. We fear the demands that force a child into sin rather than risk ridicule. Well, the Bible has something to offer us; it talks about having the kind of independence and integrity that doesn't depend upon the approval of others. When faced with gossip or ridicule, this spirit doesn't give way to an identity crisis.

> Princes also did sit and speak against me: but thy servant did *meditate in thy statutes. Thy testimonies* also are my *delight* and *my counsellors* (Ps. 119:23, 24).
>
> So shall I have wherewith to answer him that reproacheth me: *for I trust in thy word* (Ps. 119:42).
>
> The proud have had me greatly in derision: yet have I not declined from *thy law*. I remembered *thy judgments* of old, O Lord; and have comforted myself (Ps. 119:51, 52).

Here's a description of a personality strongly independent in the face of criticism from important people. Scorn and ridicule do not weaken convictions or identity, because this personality is rooted in a higher authority than public opinion—the Word of God. I guess you could call that independent self-confidence, and it's the balancing factor to popularity in a peer group. As you teach your child the Word, you are giving him the potential to be popular without compromise.

Purity Amid Perversion

Talking about popularity immediately brings to mind the spiritual and moral growth of a child. In mothers' Bible studies, I've noticed this to be a prime concern: the openness of sin in our high schools. The availability of drugs in their bathrooms is shocking to us, even if it is not to our teens. We can hardly imagine sitting in class with students who are high on grass, or drunk, and teachers who use four-letter words. Neither can our horrified minds imagine kids living in that atmosphere without participating in it. Well, they can't—unless they have two power sources operating at a daily level, and in great concentration. Those two power sources are the Holy Spirit and the Word of God. (I'm assuming, now, that these are Christian kids.) The beginning of purity in an impure world is the cleansing blood of Jesus. But the continuation of it is in the Word of God. Here's that promise, probably already familiar to you:

> Wherewithal shall a young man *cleanse his way?* by taking heed thereto *according to thy word.* With my whole heart have I sought thee; O let me not wander from thy commandments. *Thy word* have I hid in mine heart, *that I might not sin against thee* (Ps. 119:9-11).

Now, let's get more specific and look at the area of sexual purity, that old-fashioned virtue of chastity. Non-Christian parents have given up hope of it altogether. "Kids will be kids!" or "He's just sowing his wild oats"—as if rationalizing would do away with sin. Today's mothers don't expect their daughters to keep virginity; they simply provide them with contraceptives. And even Christian mothers are wondering about the resistance power of their teenage boys, when they see the seductiveness and boldness of these well-instructed girls. How much temptation can a Christian boy take?

> My son, keep thy father's commandment, and forsake not the law of thy mother; bind them continually upon thine heart, and tie them about thy neck. When thou goest, it shall lead thee;

when thou sleepest, it shall keep thee; and when thou awakest, it shall talk with thee. For the commandment is a lamp; and the *law is light; and reproofs of instruction are the way of life: to keep thee from the evil woman*, from the flattery of the tongue of a strange woman. Lust not after her beauty in thine heart; neither let her take thee with her eyelids. For by means of a whorish woman a man is brought to a piece of bread. . . . Can a man take fire in his bosom, and not be burned? (Prov. 6:20-27).

Have you ever read that with your son? It could make a difference some starry night! In fact, if you have boys, the first seven chapters of Proverbs should be read every few months. Or girls, for that matter! Girls will receive them differently, but just as effectively, because they contain descriptions of seductive women and God's scornful attitude toward them. When a girl gets those pictures deep into her heart, the playboy bunnies begin to look less glamorous! But without the Word of God, a girl growing up in our television-controlled society will quite naturally come to think of herself as a sex object. *Cosmopolitan* magazine interviewed a wealthy prostitute who complained that her profession was languishing for customers because of the multitudes of stupid girls "giving it out for free." Her scorn for these "immoral" girls was only as paradoxical as the whole interview, done by a magazine devoted to making promiscuity sophisticated, a magazine which makes its appeal to high school and college girls.

With propaganda like this endeavoring to convince our girls that it's neat to be indiscreet, very few are getting any knowledge of what the Bible says. I frequently meet Christian girls who grew up with the idea that adultery was wrong—unfaithfulness to a man you're married to—but reasoned that sex before marriage was all right because you weren't being unfaithful to anyone. Many of them had never heard of fornication, or been taught the commandments against it. One girl from a Christian family described her sex education as a nervous talk with her mother. "You know what's right and you know what's wrong. And you know what happens to girls who do wrong!" Isn't that terrific! That girl was hearing the arguments of her boyfriend as to why every girl should experience sex *before* marriage. They sounded much more logical than her mother; and, not knowing the Scripture said anything more than "God created them male and female" (which of course, the *boys* could quote!), she indulged in experiences she was truly sorry for later.

One summer day I was scheduled to speak at a nearby youth camp to teenage girls about sex and marriage. As usual, I packed up large charts with lists of scripture verses on them, and drove to camp with my nine-year-old daughter. Carmen had a friend whose parents managed the camp, and she was planning to play with Carolyn, but Carolyn was not there. Thinking of my "adult" subject, I said, "Carmen, why don't you take a nice hike or swing awhile?"

"No, Mom, I think I'll go sit with the big girls in your class."

What could I say? "This is a naughty subject and we don't want you to hear about it"? So I said nothing, and imagined she'd get bored after the first ten minutes and go play. But there she sat, for the whole hour, listening intently to all those explicit scriptures and to the comments and questions of the girls (who, by the way, were beautiful and receptive to the Word).

Driving home that night, I had second thoughts; should I have let her stay? was she too young to be exposed to such a talk? But soon after we arrived home, I concluded the Lord must have planned the events of the day; maybe He knew my child's need better than I did. Alone in the house, we turned on the TV set, "Marcus Welby, M.D." Would you believe, the program that night was about a nice teenage girl who let herself be used and contracted venereal disease. A story so Christian in its whole approach and in Dr. Welby's talks with the girl, it could have been shown in a church. As we watched, and Carmen asked questions, it became apparent she'd thoroughly understood the scriptures we'd just studied. She got a healthy, well-dramatized sex education in one day, through no real fault of my own!

It wasn't until later that I saw the significance of this. I knew the Lord had engineered it, but why? It came out that a hypocritical babysitter (we thought she was a Christian) had explained the facts of life to Carmen from her own perverted viewpoint, telling her that all boys and girls have sexual relations when they go on dates. Carmen, thinking this girl a Christian, was carrying around a horrible misconception. But the Lord used a group of real Christian girls to destroy that misconception, while letting her own mother teach her the Scriptures! This turned out to be important as she entered fourth grade, where children with older brothers and sisters seemed to take it upon themselves to educate the rest in *their* strange misinformation! Thanks to the content of the Word in her life, she knew the true from the false.

Let's continue discussion, now, on *spiritual and moral growth*. Besides purity and protection in temptation, the Scripture also relates several other values to knowledge of the Word: the favor of God, right paths (guidance and direction), counseling, correction, and honesty.

Guidance and direction for a child's life are not something *you* can give forever. Legally, at 21 at least, you no longer have that privilege. And even during the last of the teen years, your advice is sometimes not appreciated! We need to provide the equipment for continuous, accurate guidance. Otherwise we're turning him loose in a car that has no steering wheel! "You're on your own now!" "You'll have to make your own decisions." "It's your life—do whatever you want with it." What frightening words those are to an 18-year-old who's never been taught to drive! The antidote to that kind of fear is right here:

> Let thine heart retain my words; keep my commandments, and live. . . . I have taught thee in the way of wisdom; I have led thee in *right paths*. When thou goest, thy steps shall not be straitened; and when thou runnest, thou shalt not stumble (Prov. 4:4, 11, 12).

The Word of God is the compass, the steering wheel.

It's the equipment we must provide. We need to teach him to drive the car. If we succeed, he'll be saved a lot of miserable stumbling, groping for his goals and purposes, finding only after years of trial and error what he really wants to do with his life. There *are* people over forty still trying to make that very basic decision. Both Jerry and I experienced the Bible as a guide that will prevent groping. We were blessed with a childhood rich in the Word of God, and it paid off when the time came to make those decisions about careers and marriage. Praise the Lord for making all our adult years productive ones and not aimless wandering! Someone advised me early in my Christian life (ten years old), "Read a chapter of the Bible every night." I did that, for all the nights I can remember from then on—and for many of those high school years, I made a practice of memorizing a verse a night. I fully believe that habit was tied to the fact that at seventeen I knew with no doubts what profession I was to pursue, what college to attend, and what to major in. Jerry, living in another part of the country, experienced the same explicit direction in those decisions. That wonderful, accurate guidance continued in choosing a seminary, a home, a church to pastor. And it's always operated through the Word, often in terms of specific scriptures, such as the one which nearly named the little church we were to choose as our first (and, so far, last!)—East Hill.

Part of guidance is correction. Suppose a child makes a wrong decision, or refuses the guidance he's already received?

> I thought on my ways, and turned my feet unto thy testimonies. I made haste, and delayed not to keep thy commandments (Ps. 119:59, 60).

It's a funny picture, if you'll visualize it. Imagine your nineteen-year-old son driving at night in unfamiliar territory. He realizes he's not driving on the road at all, but in some farmer's field! (That happened to us one dark night in an unpopulated area of Washington, and, believe me, we made haste to get back on the road!)

But there's an assumption here, that the driver knows about the road, and he can tell when he gets off it. If a child goes wrong in his decisions, the Word of God will correct him quickly—*provided* you've placed it in his life! He will know when he's off the road, and he will turn his feet unto God's testimonies, having known about them and experienced them before.

Counselling is related to this; that is, guidance and direction. The Word of God is the ultimate counselor, far more dependable than the school guidance counselor or even the Christian psychiatrist.

In college, an advisor assigned to my husband misunderstood Jerry's goals. He had mapped a course of study that would have led to a degree he didn't want. When a new counselor was assigned, it was discovered that he would have taken many unnecessary courses, while leaving out the necessary ones. Thank God there was a better Counselor at work, who led Jerry to inquire into the situation before it became hopeless. Another counselor at the same fine Christian college advised him to drop his ambition to enter the ministry. What a tragedy that would have been! And yet there were many students who made lifetime decisions on the advice of that learned professor!

Human counselors are needed and valuable. But for my children, I want a more sure guide. Their fortunes don't need to rise and fall on the mistakes of the "experts." "Thy testimonies are my delight and *my counsellors*" (Ps. 119:24). When a child can say *that*, he can throw the advice of experts against the Word and get an answer back. He can recognize scriptural advice when he hears it, and ungodly advice will be discarded.

Now, the last point of spiritual and moral development I'll mention is honesty. Is it true that all children cheat in school, and that *all* children lie when they're sure they won't get caught? Well, only if you listen to the opinions of those who do! You reprimand Linda when you find she's cheating on a book report. Her answer is, of course, "All the other kids do it!" And if you're a typical mother, you respond, "I don't care if all the other kids *do*, it doesn't make it right!" But inside you wonder if you're holding an impossible standard, and all 33 sixth graders actually do cheat. Let me reassure you: they don't! In an average group, some will cheat at every chance; others only occasionally, and many, not at all. It's the _perpetual cheaters_ who justify themselves by trying to indict everyone; that's a good clue to remember when you get that story! There are many kids in school, not even from Christian homes, who are scrupulously taught honesty and live it. How much more should children of Christian parents be students of integrity. Notice, however, the importance of the Word of God in these verses about truthfulness:

> I hate and abhor lying, but _thy law do I love_ (Ps. 119:163).
> Remove from me the way of lying: and grant me _thy law_ graciously. I have chosen the way of truth; thy judgments have I laid before me (Ps. 119:29, 30).

It's one thing to tell a child, "Always tell the truth"; it's another, to put truth into his life. When he loves the Word, he will hate and abhor lying.

Have Your Own Bible Study

Take Out a Real Life Insurance Policy

Earlier we declared that a knowledge of the Word of God is like a marvelous insurance policy, with the best possible coverage. Here, now, is a list of the benefits we've just described:

When you give a child knowledge of the Word of God, you give him:

I. _Mental Development_
   1. Common sense (wisdom): Prov. 1:2.
   2. Comprehension (understanding): Ps. 119:130; Prov. 1:2.
   3. Intelligence (subtilty): Prov. 1:3, 4.
   4. Knowledge: Prov. 1:4.

II. _Physical Development_
   1. Life: Prov. 3:2.
   2. Health: Prov. 4:20-22.
   3. Long life: Prov. 3:2.

III. *Emotional Development*
1. Peace: Prov. 3:1, 2; Ps. 119:165.
2. Cheerful outlook (hope): Ps. 119:49, 50.
3. Comfort: Ps. 119:49, 50.
4. Quickening (enthusiasm, alertness, motivation): Ps. 119:25, 40, 50, 88, 93, 107, 154.
5. Liberty—freedom from emotional hang-ups: Ps. 119:44, 45.
6. Delight: Ps. 119:24.
7. Joy

IV. *Social Development*
1. Favor with men (popularity; respect of peers; good reputation): Prov. 3:1-4.
2. Independent, self-confidence; identity: Ps. 119:23, 24, 42, 51, 52.

V. *Spiritual and Moral Development*
1. God's favor: Prov. 3:1, 3.
2. Right paths (guidance and direction): Prov. 4:4-12.
3. Purity: Ps. 119:9-11.
4. Protection in temptation and stress: Prov. 6:6-27.
5. Counselling: Ps. 119:24.
6. Correction: Ps. 119:59, 60.
7. Honesty: Ps. 119:29, 30, 163.

SECTION 2

Training Your Child to Love and Serve God

Chapter 7

Bring Your Child to Jesus

Do you remember the mothers in the Bible who brought their babies to Jesus? Wouldn't you love to have been among them? I think those children lived their lives with the glory of that touch! As adults, they could look back and say, "One day, when I was just a little tot, my mother took me to Jesus. Think of that! He laid His hands on me and blessed me. He received me. He accepted me, even as a child." Can your children say that? "My mother brought me to Jesus." Many teens are saying things like, "I never knew who Jesus was until this year," or, "Our family didn't go to any church. My parents didn't want me to feel they'd forced religion on me. They said I could choose the faith I wanted when I was old enough." And even many who consider themselves Christian parents have not brought their children to Jesus. They've sent them to a Sunday school that teaches how to have good manners and love your neighbor, but not one where Jesus is known and loved. It's possible to send or take children to church without taking them to Jesus. Observing parents' religion is not the same as an encounter with a living Christ.

Some adults have the attitude that children are unable to experience or understand spiritual things. This is common even among committed Christians, and it was the mistaken attitude of the disciples surrounding Jesus. Remember how they pushed the children away? "Get out of here, you noisy brats! Jesus has important things to do!" How tragic that it's often *our* reaction to the little kids running around, getting underfoot in our churches.

"They brought babies for him to touch: but when the disciples saw them they scolded them for it. But Jesus called for the children and said, 'Let the little ones come to me: do not try to stop them: for the Kingdom of God belongs to such as these. I tell you that whoever does not accept the Kingdom of God like a child will never enter it' " (Luke 18:15-17). In Mark's account, it says that Jesus was openly disgusted with their attitude, angry: "They brought children for him to touch: and the disciples scolded them for it. But when Jesus saw this he was *indignant*, and said to them, 'Let the children come to me: do not try to stop them: for the Kingdom of God belongs to such as these. I tell you, whoever does not accept the Kingdom of God like a child will never enter it.' And he put his arms around them, laid his hands upon them, and blessed them" (Mark 10:13-16). Matthew's account emphasizes the *reason* these mothers brought the children. It wasn't just a sight-seeing trip. "They brought children for him *to lay his hands on them with prayer.* The disciples scolded them for it, but Jesus said to them, 'Let the children come to me: do not try to stop them: for the Kingdom of Heaven belongs to such as these.' And he laid his hands on the children, and went his way" (Matt. 18:1-7).

Visualize the mothers, the children, Jesus, and the disciples, with their four different attitudes. The parents had the right idea; Jesus was pleased to answer their request. This act of faith was done in *public*, just as Jewish babies were presented publicly to the Lord in the temple. This is one reason many churches encourage parents to dedicate babies. It's a public statement of their commitment to raise a child in the love of God. It's also a time they can point the child back to, as we've been able to say to our children, "This is a picture of you on the day you were dedicated to the Lord. You were only a month old when we took you to the church, and, with our big Christian family looking on, we asked the Lord to be in charge of your life. Ever since that day, He's been taking care of you and working in your life." This is one part, and most likely the first part, of bringing a child to Jesus. Very early in his life, you ask Jesus to lay His hands on him and bless him with that special touch.

This particular story of Jesus and the children has been the focus of many happy times in our home. We had a modern version of the event in the form of a colored picture. For years it hung on a wall of the girls' bedroom, especially placed so their eyes fell on it when they got into bed. When I first hung it, they had interesting questions. The children in this picture are dressed in our kind of clothing, and they're showing Jesus their toy airplane and climbing on His lap. It beautifully shows how Jesus cares about children and is interested in every part of their lives. One of the discussions was that as those mommies brought their children to Jesus, Christi and Carmen were brought to Jesus at a very early age as Mommy and Daddy dedicated them to Him at the church. Another was that some day we'd see Him face to face as those children did. I can still remember Christi saying, "When I see Jesus, I'm going to give Him a great big kiss!"

Another story we've enjoyed is the story of Samuel, whose mother took him to the temple and gave him to serve the Lord there all his life. And of course, how God spoke to Samuel and used him mightily at even a young age. We say, "Of course, we didn't leave you at the church, did we? But, we did give you to God, and we did ask Him to use you and help you serve Him all your life."

When Samuel was about to retire, he had this wonderful testimony when he stood before Israel: "I have walked before you from my childhood unto this day. Behold, here I am: witness against me before the Lord, and before his anointed: whose ox have I taken? ... or whom have I defrauded?" (1 Sam. 12:2, 3). Samuel had lived such a godly life from his childhood to old age that not one person could charge him with sin. That's the testimony I'd love to see my children have—to have walked with the Lord from childhood on, not having to experiment with sin before they really come to Christ; but just starting to learn about Jesus at the toddler age and responding to Him continuously, growing in grace and in commitment to Him as the years go by. Adults who have that kind of testimony are free from many hang-ups and from the backlash of sin. They don't regret for a minute that they've never experienced drugs or drunkenness or free sex. They were brought to Jesus by parents who dedicated them to Him and they've found Him a loving Lord, too good to leave for a rebellious life.

When you can point a child back to a time like his dedication, a public event at a point in time, you give him an awareness of his importance to you. Also he has an inner security knowing the Lord is really in charge of him. As he grows into adolescence and strives for independence from his parents, that knowledge of belonging to the Lord can give him a real anchor. Deep inside he knows, "I'm not just anybody. I've been given to the Lord—marked for His Kingdom. No matter what I do, I'll never be able to escape that!"

In many churches a public dedication is such a common event that we allow it to lose its meaning. In fact, some parents don't even bother with it, feeling that it's nothing more than a ritual involving an infant with no spiritual understanding anyway! I've been more and more impressed with the importance of this act as our children are coming into a world where satanism and witchcraft are increasing. It's essential that Christian parents make sure the first spiritual force a child experiences is that of Jesus. Yes, it *is* a ritual, but one full of life and meaning. It is an announcement to God, to the church, and to the devil that you intend this child to be raised for God's Kingdom.

In Bible days, Jewish children were presented to God. All around them, heathen children were dedicated to the demonic gods and goddesses served by their parents. Some children were even sacrificed to these monstrous idols. Can you imagine the delight of Satan when pagan parents came with the precious new baby God had just made, stood before a statue of Diana and said, "Great Goddess Diana, we dedicate this child to you!" The Bible says these idols each had a demon behind them. As they were worshipped, people opened themselves to demon activity. There is evidence that there are evil forces involved in astrology—their guidance from Taurus the Bull, Pisces and Leo the Lion. Satan in this way gets an open invitation to govern that person's life, and is he thrilled!

Now, the Jewish people viewed the Gentiles as unclean because they had been presented to Satan at birth. But Paul wrote some interesting things in 1 Corinthians 7:14, applying to Christians caught in a situation where only one parent had accepted Christ: "For the unbelieving husband is sanctified by the wife, and the unbelieving wife is sanctified by the husband: else were your children unclean: but now are they holy."

You see, part of the problem husbands and wives were having at that time was that adults who had once been offered to idols now were coming to Jesus. Let's imagine you have come to Jesus and your husband hasn't. You may be among the women who have wondered if they should leave their husbands, since to remain joined to him is to be yoked to a child of Satan. And suppose the children of your marriage have been presented to demons? Imagine the remorse you would feel were you a mother now coming to Jesus! So Paul wrote these comforting words, "If a woman has an unbelieving husband who consents to live with her, she should not leave him. For the unbelieving husband is, so to speak, sanctified by the believing wife, and the unbelieving wife is sanctified by the believing husband. Otherwise the children born would be unclean, whereas now they are holy." Now that doesn't mean your husband and children are automatically saved because of your relationship to Christ. They have to make that decision for themselves. But it does mean that, to some extent anyway, they're protected from the workings of Satan for your sake, and they've been set aside for special attention from the Holy Spirit. In light of this, it seems to me doubly important that a mother married to an unsaved man present her children to the Lord. Don't wait until he becomes a

Christian. Your babies need, right now, all the protection they can get since spiritual leadership is missing in their father. A child dedicated to the Lord as soon as he's born into this kind of home will grow up with a different personality and with less pressure from the devil than if you wait until he's four or five when his father has finally given up his stubbornness. Do it publicly, in your church. You need the support and love of that congregation for your child. When you do it publicly, you mean business. You're saying, "Lord, here I am, in front of all these people, asking you to take charge of this child. I'm declaring that I will raise him to love you, and I'm asking the help of my brothers and sisters." God will hold you to that. He doesn't take a public vow lightly. For your child's sake and your own, you need to make that step.

Can a Child Know God?

I wondered a little when my four-year-old came to me and said, just out of the blue, "Mommy, pray with me. I want to take Jesus as my Saviour."

"O Lord, give me wisdom! What about these childhood decisions? Does she really know what it's all about?" Well, she did! The years have borne that out, and I'm so glad I didn't discourage her.

Remember how God talked to the little boy Samuel? At first even the High Priest Eli didn't understand what was going on. After the third time, he got the message. "It's not me calling you, son. It's God. Next time He speaks your name, ask Him what He wants you to know." Samuel did, and God gave him a word of prophecy that was detailed and complete, though probably not fully understandable to a small boy. Every word of that prophecy came to pass, exactly as Samuel had stated it!

Mother, you may never know until your child is grown about the relationship he's developing with God right now. His young lips can't always verbalize it, but if you've brought him to Jesus, first as a baby, then as a toddler, as a kindergartner and a first grader, you can be sure Jesus is responding to him as he's responding to Jesus.

You may find you need to study enough to satisfy your own mind in answer to this question, "Can a child know God?" In that case, here are passages which I feel indicate that a child can have a very real friendship with God. Some of them are discussed in other chapters: Matt. 18:1-7, 10; Luke 18:15-17; Mark 10:13-16; 1 Sam. 3, 4; Ps. 8:2; Matt. 21:15-16.

This verse in Matthew 21 came to have special meaning to me when our son Jamie was born: "Out of the mouths of babes and sucklings thou hast perfected praise." That's really mind-boggling! Even babies can praise the Lord!

Jamie went down in medical records as the "sickest baby we've ever saved." Those were the doctor's words when it was all over. Our pediatrician was asked to write a full report for the Medical Association explaining the complicated machinery and treatments he had developed in the process of "saving Jamie."

From the nurses to the interns, we all knew we'd been involved in a miracle. Jamie was a "Karen Quinlan" case—kept alive on a respirator. His lungs were filled with meconium, a sticky substance that could not be pumped out. The X-rays were whited out —he was alive only mechanically.

In the dark and frightening hours of the most hopeless night, the Lord spoke to Jerry and told him to read Psalm 30. In words similar to this, He comforted Jerry, "The spirit of your baby is crying out to me, and I hear him. Psalm 30 is the content of his prayer. He is praising me for victory over death." To you, that may sound like the imagination of a desperate father, but look at what we read in that Psalm

"I will extol thee, O Lord; for thou hast lifted me up, and hast not made my foes to rejoice over me. O Lord my God, I cried unto thee, and thou hast healed me. O Lord, thou hast brought up my soul from the grave: thou hast kept me alive, that I should not go down to the pit. Sing unto the Lord, O ye saints of his, and give thanks at the remembrance of his holiness. . . . I cried to thee, O Lord; and unto the Lord I made supplication. What profit is there in my blood, when I go down to the pit? Shall the dust praise thee? shall it declare thy truth? Hear, O Lord, and have mercy upon me: Lord, be thou my helper. Thou has turned for me my mourning into dancing: thou hast put off my sackcloth, and girded me with gladness; to the end that my glory may sing praise to thee, and not be silent. O Lord my God, I will give thanks unto thee forever" (Ps. 30:1-4, 8-12).

When we took our baby home from the hospital twelve days later, it was with a clean bill of health and clear lungs. The nurses wept for joy with us as we dressed him to go home. The most impossible baby of all had become a miracle of God.

Around a year later, we visited in a home where a large picture of Jesus hung on the wall—a rugged, profile portrait that is not often seen. The moment Jamie entered, he ran to the picture with this ecstatic look on his face as though he were meeting a long-time friend. "Jesus!" he said excitedly. "Hi, Jesus!"

I asked the girls, "How did he know that was Jesus? Have you ever shown him a picture like that?" We didn't have a picture of Jesus on our wall at that time. In fact, I didn't know he could say "Jesus"—we were just starting in on "Mama" and "Dadda"! Could it be that the picture was a close likeness to the Jesus whom Jamie had already seen?

Mother's Part

The second step in bringing your child into a personal relationship with the Saviour begins when you start teaching him to pray. Very early, by a year old if he's learning to talk, he's learning to talk to his friend Jesus, just as he learns to talk with you. I can remember feeding the cereal to our first baby every morning before dashing off to teach school. She must have been about ten months old and sitting on my lap at the table. I could never be in too much of a hurry to skip the breakfast prayer. She simply sat with her eyes closed and hands folded until we had prayed. Not long after that, she would say, along with me, "Dear Jesus." In that sense of daily relationship with

Him, a child can be brought to Jesus by his mother, who teaches him to know God and communicate with Him. Never underestimate that! God does talk to children. He communicates in ways they can understand.

In view of this, it seems only wise to encourage any response a child makes to God, at any age. If he wants to pray, give, worship, why shouldn't he? Let him respond to Jesus every time he wants. Don't put down his faith. "Whoever causes one of these little ones who believe in me to stumble, it is better for him that a heavy millstone be hung around his neck, and that he be drowned in the depth of the sea." It sounds as if the judgment on skeptics who discourage children is going to be harsh! I wouldn't want to be in that group!

Jesus Touches Today's Children

There are many aspects to this concept of bringing your child to Jesus. Bring your child to Jesus at birth in gratitude, bring him for salvation at an early age. Then, bring him daily to Jesus in prayer. Bring him to Jesus when he has a problem. Bring him for healing if he has a physical need. Many children live with health problems that Jesus would like to heal.

Friends of mine have a boy who was born with a congenital heart defect. The story of how he was healed is the story of a child's faith reaching out to a Saviour he knew loved him. It's also a hilarious story, because the boy had two skeptical parents to contend with. Even when they saw him healed with their own eyes at a Kathryn Kuhlman meeting, they didn't believe! Well, they do now! It's been several years, and that boy is in no way similar to the invalid they half-heartedly took to the meeting.

Many families in our congregation have brought a child to Jesus and seen him made whole. One Sunday night, Sam and Annie brought their boy for prayer. He had a serious hearing problem, and the doctor recommended surgery. Just a few minutes after prayer, Patrick was sitting in the service with his parents. He put both hands over his ears and whispered,

"Mommy, why are they singing so loud tonight?" Needless to say, he didn't have to go through surgery!

Our daughter was healed from what should have killed her—crib death. Fast-thinking grandparents prayed the prayer of faith immediately. Then miraculously, a plug of mucous that had blocked the flow of oxygen to the brain just disintegrated and came pouring out her nose on the way to the hospital. The doctors were mystified, but later we understood that Jesus had saved her life. It would have been too late at the hospital. Even so, the doctors were convinced there was brain damage. If there was, the Lord healed that too. We prayed about that, and in the nine years that have elapsed, her intelligence has been unquestioned and the brain wave tests show no damage. I'm so glad we had a Saviour to bring our child to in that moment; and that when my children have any kind of a need, I can bring them to Jesus. I may not have the answer, but He does!

The New Testament is full of parents bringing their children to Jesus. Some, like Jairus' daughter, were all but dead. Whatever the need, Jesus healed the child. There was one qualification: you had to come. Lots of sick children living in Galilee never got healed, though Jesus was near their homes. The ones He touched were the ones whose parents had the faith to bring them. All through Scripture you see this principle at work—children receiving from Jesus on the basis of the faith of their parents. Sometimes a spiritual battle ensues, and parents must use the weapons of spiritual warfare to defeat the enemy who hates children. Sometimes there's a time lapse between prayer and medical evidence, as in the case of the ten lepers. The child might not understand what's going on, but the parents' faith will win out. God will honor it.

Many Christian mothers think the essential thing is to bring a child to Jesus for salvation; that is, seeing that he makes a personal decision for Christ. That's important, but when this decision is based on a life-style of bringing your child to Jesus it has real depth and meaning. That life-style can begin even before birth, and it can continue on a daily basis until a precious relationship has formed with the Saviour.

Your Child and Your Church

If it's true that your child can know the Lord and have a real, vital walk with Him, then your church and all that takes place there becomes a serious consideration. Is your church enhancing or discouraging your child's walk with God? Are the people he's fellowshipping with the kind of Christians who will give him an accurate picture of Christ? Are they people who love him and minister to his needs, answer his questions and pray with him? Do they view him as a person with capacity for spiritual growth, or merely a kid who needs entertaining while Mom and Dad are "in church," doing the "real things"? (If you're a Sunday school teacher or children's church worker, those are questions to ask of yourself.) Jesus had serious things to say about those who shape the lives of children. Not only did He believe they were capable of a close relationship to God, He called them "These little ones who believe in me" and warned of severe punishment to anyone who damaged their faith: "Whoso shall receive one such little child in my name receiveth me. But whoso shall offend one of these little ones which believe in me, it were better for him that a millstone were hanged about his neck, and that he were drowned in the depth of the sea" (Matt. 18:5, 6).

I'm repeating this verse here because it has such heavy implications to our churches. We dare not treat our children as spectators to our worship, our teaching and singing. They're part of the Body of Christ. They, so vulnerable and so valuable, are the little ones who believe. We must never harm them by underrating their faith.

If you read the four Gospels through noting the times children are mentioned, you'll be surprised to see how large a part they played in Jesus' ministry. Many children were involved in face-to-face encounters with Jesus: when He personally singled out a little girl and healed her, when He accepted a gift from a little boy who wanted to give Him some bread and fish. Children were in the throngs that gathered to hear Him preach. Children were praising Him in the temple and children were shouting "Hosanna" as He rode into Jerusalem. Children found Jesus approachable, interesting and loving. There was no need for them to be mere spectators to "adult" events.

The Church of Today

So often we hear it said, "Our children are the church of tomorrow." No, they're not! They're the church of *today*! Membership in the Body of Christ is not determined by age; it's determined by your relationship to Jesus. When you have the idea that children or teens are the church of tomorrow, everything that's done for them will be in terms of preparing them for some day in the future when they'll be old enough to *really* worship, pray and witness. They'll be babysat in Sunday school classes that are merely supervised playtimes, then later in a succession of parties and clubs designed to "hold them," keep them in the church so they won't go "into the world." But if they're the church of today, they'll be allowed to minister in the church. The Sunday school classes will be actual ministering times when four-year-olds pray for one another and worship the Lord, when junior highers are not spectators to be entertained but growing Christians digging into the Word together, sharing their needs, praising and giving testimony. Teenagers won't be "held in the church" by a cute club that gives them fun and games but by genuine commitment to Jesus Christ and His Body. They'll go to church because the services minister to them, not because the youth director entertains them.

Here's what the New Testament says about young people: "And it shall come to pass in the last days, saith God, I will pour out of my Spirit upon all flesh: and your sons and your daughters shall prophesy, and your young men shall see visions, and your old men shall dream dreams: and on my servants and on my handmaidens I will pour out in those days of my Spirit: and they shall prophesy" (Acts 2:17, 18). That's how the Holy Spirit can come into the lives of your sons and your daughters. He empowers them with supernatural gifts. They become dynamic ministers to the world, right along with the Spirit-filled pastors and teachers. That passage shows that we, the last-day church, should be producing young men and women who know how to stand and prophesy. That cannot take place when adult Christians have the idea that youth are the church of tomorrow. Kids who *could* prophesy won't if it's assumed they're too young. Maybe that's why Paul had to reassure Timothy. He said, Timothy, "let no man despise thy youth; but be thou an example of the believers" (1 Tim. 4:12). Evidently that's possible, even in the middle of growing pains, acne and high school, or the Word wouldn't encourage it!

The early church was made up of people of all ages. Some of its bravest leaders were young men, many probably in their teens. These kids had the same immaturities that kids have today. The early church was reaching *young people* because it was preaching the Gospel to *people*. Children and teenagers are people. As the Holy Spirit empowered the preaching with signs and miracles, *people* accepted Jesus—little people and big people, Greeks and Jews, blacks and whites, children and adults. Sometimes it amazes me to see how the Lord works in our group. He'll use a college boy to minister to an old lady, or a small child to win a teenager.

I asked a young man who was having a tremendous time at a pastors' conference, "How did you happen to come?" (He was not a pastor, by any stretch of the imagination!) Wendell told me about someone named Emma whom he had met near the conference site. Her dynamic Christian life and love so impressed him that he just had to sneak in and meet other Christians like her. Now I happen to know Emma, and she's past seventy years old! The Lord used her to minister to this teenage vagabond who was camped near us. Wendell accepted Jesus, and every day that week he crawled out of his tent and trudged down the mountain to worship and study with us.

A junior high class in our church decorated their wall with a collage entitled, "The Church: The Body of Christ." In the collage were pictures of people—young married couples, old men, little girls with pigtails, teenage boys in dungarees, grandmothers and grandfathers. When a church looks like that, it's a beautiful sight. And when it does, it's because all these people are ministered to in it. To have a Body like that takes a lot of love and tolerance for different life-styles; for the differences in tastes and cultures of varied generations, it means unconditional acceptance of every brother or sister in the Body, regardless of age.

Have Your Own Bible Study

Bring Your Child to Jesus

What does the Bible say:
1. About children and their relationships with God?
   See Matt. 18:1-7, 10; Mark 10:13-16; Luke 18:15-17; 1 Sam. 3:4; Ps. 8:2; Matt. 21:15, 16; 1 Cor. 7:14.
2. About teenagers in the Body of Christ?
   See Acts 2:17; 1 Tim. 4:12.

Chapter 8

Habits and Attitudes for Healthy Christians

If you're a Christian mother, I'm sure you're doing everything possible to encourage your children to become Christians. You understand the eternal value of a relationship with Jesus Christ and you want it for your child. But I'd like you to think about a goal beyond even that. I certainly do want my children to grow up to be Christian adults, but even more I want them to be committed, mature, Spirit-filled Christians who experience the real joy and rewards of knowing Jesus. Did you know that you equip a child with certain habits and attitudes that seriously affect the quality of his Christian life as an adult? It's worth putting some thought into and deciding just what habits you'll choose to teach, just as you choose to teach a child habits of eating and sleeping, brushing his teeth and making his bed. If you're like most of us, you don't have to make a big decision every morning on whether to brush your teeth or not! That daily decision was made for you long ago when your mother stood you on a stool in front of the sink and trained you in a healthful habit. Likewise, we can provide our children with habits that will greatly simplify consistent Christian living. One of them is the regular habit of reading the Bible each day.

Consistent study of the Bible is as essential to spiritual growth as daily meat and potatoes are to physical growth. The New Testament instructs us and our children, "As newborn babes, desire the sincere milk of the word, that ye may grow thereby" (1 Pet. 2:2). At this point you are able to predict at least one thing with reasonable certainty about your little boy's life as an adult—he will sit down and eat food each day! You've helped him form the habit of breakfast, lunch and supper. But what about the nutrition he's going to need for a healthy spiritual life? Wouldn't it be easier for him to maintain if he had spent many years with a habit of feeding upon the Word of God? If you are used to spending time in the Scriptures every day and suddenly you don't have that, don't you find that you get hungry? I really do! And the next day is just like the day after I go off my diet—I eat twice as much! You see, the Word of God is alive. It has a quality of energy and vitality that you don't find in any other piece of literature—energy that affects even a child.

I was led to Christ at the age of ten by my Sunday school teachers, Mr. and Mrs. Livingston. They instructed me to read at least a chapter of the Bible every day. So, I began in Genesis and read straight through to Revelation, a chapter or two each night at bedtime. That habit turned out to be the most stabilizing force in my life as I went through high school and college. I'm sure I understood almost nothing in Exodus or Leviticus at such a young age, but the habit stuck, even through those mysterious books. It was the beginning of my gaining a firm grasp on the Word.

There are five fingers on the hand with which you hold your Bible, and to hold it firmly, you need to use all five of them. If you will visualize those five fingers, with a small label stuck on each one, you can understand the five elements needed by a child for a firm grip of the Bible. Let's label your thumb Number 1: *Reading the Bible*—that's as basic as your thumb is to gripping anything. But even a thumb is useless without Number 2: an index finger. And so, along with reading the Bible we need to *meditate upon it*, think about what it's saying to us, to *understand* what we read. Number 3 in our picture of the five fingers is to *memorize the Word*. Number 4 is a *systematic study* of the

Word. Number 5 is the *application* of the Word to our lives. Those five things should be part of a habit of Bible study in a child's life. They can all be incorporated into your family life. And this is what happens in a good Sunday school class. The teacher helps children *read* the Bible, *meditate* upon it together (think about it and discuss it), *memorize* key verses, *study it in a systematic way*, and then *apply* it with real life illustrations about children their age going to school, playing with friends and using the Scriptures as a guide. You see, that's what Sunday school is all about. It's designed to build a habit of Bible study into your child!

Attitudes Are Habit Forming and Habits Are Attitude-Forming!

When we talk about habits, we have to talk about attitudes. The way in which you train a habit will determine either a negative or positive attitude. Attitudes are habit-forming themselves. Also, habits are "attitude-forming." It's difficult to discuss either one without the other. Just by developing the habit of spending time in the Scriptures each day, we plant the attitude within a child that says the Bible is important—it's something special—and we plant the attitude that views the Word of God as a dependable authority for living.

Our example is contagious. If our children see us studying, memorizing and consulting the Bible, they will have the beginning of the habit. Little Rebecca could hardly wait to learn to read, because she was dying to find out what was in that big black book she saw her mother read so often!

Now do you catch the basic concept? I've tried to illustrate it by talking about Bible study, but we could just as easily discuss the habits of prayer, worship, fellowship, tithing, giving—and we'll get into some of those areas in this chapter. Here we've talked about the habit of Bible study, but the corresponding attitude that I want for my children is a *love* for the Word of God. To study it as a painful duty and a dry ritual is not enough. And so, along with the training of the habit, we're trying to do things in such a way that our children will have the feeling that David expressed in these verses from Psalm 119 (all are good verses, by the way, to use for a child's memorization):

I will delight myself in thy statutes: I will not forget thy word (16).

Thy testimonies also are my delight and my counsellors (24).

And I will delight myself in thy commandments, which I have loved (47).

Oh how love I thy law! it is my meditation all the day (97).

How sweet are thy words unto my taste! yea, sweeter than honey to my mouth (103).

Isn't that beautiful? That's the attitude a child can have toward the Word if we'll make the effort to teach it.

Church and Worship Habits

My husband is a preacher and the son of a preacher. When Jerry was six years old, his father was called into the ministry. He sold his home, left a good job and took the family to California to enroll in Bible college. For five years, he worked as a welder, went to school nights, and through much sacrifice succeeded in becoming a pastor. When I met Jerry, his life had been entirely formed around the ministry and church. He had lived many places. He had gone to thirteen different schools in twelve years. To a small town girl like myself, who had lived in the same house in the same town all my life, it seemed impossible a child could survive all that. But here he was, well adjusted, happy, capable, and already a fine preacher himself. I noticed a certain pattern to his life. He spent time praying and reading the Scripture every day. When Sunday came, it never seemed to occur to him that there was anything else to do but go to Sunday school and church in the morning, eat dinner, then go back to the church for a youth meeting and evening service. It would be unthinkable to do anything else, even though we were carefree college students and there was no one checking to make sure we attended church. Lots of my friends sleep until noon on Sundays; but Jerry had a habit built into his life, and life would seem abnormal without it. Now my life revolves around the same habits, and I sometimes notice that to some families Sunday is just another day. I wonder what they do in it! It must be terribly lonely and boring to lay around in front of a television set all day.

I remember asking Jerry about this habit once: "Did your parents force you to go to church?" "Well, I don't think so," he said. "That's just what we did on Sundays."

Surprising though it may seem, children who grow up in church don't necessarily grow up with resentment! It doesn't need to be a grueling, boring experience. Sometimes adults torture their children in church, expecting more of them than God expects. A description of families worshipping together is found in Nehemiah 12:43: "That day they offered great sacrifices, and rejoiced: for God had made them rejoice with great joy: the wives also and the children rejoiced: so that the joy of Jerusalem was heard even afar off." Is this a description of the kind of worship your child is being exposed to? He needs to experience the joy and beauty of worshipping the Lord. He needs to be with adults and other children who are praising God and enjoying Him. If your child is merely a spectator at a service he does not understand or participate in, of course he'll grow up with a resentful attitude toward church. But if church is a place where he sees the power of God at work in saving sinners, healing the sick, and transforming lives, he's not going to have to be forced to go there. If he fellowships every week with people who love each other and love him, if he is allowed to participate, to sing the songs, pray for others and read the Scriptures along with the pastor, the habit will be an addictive one. We can see this in the lives of thousands of young people today.

One unsaved father said to me, "That boy of mine would go to church every night and day if there was something going on!" The father didn't understand it because in his days of church-going, it was one dreary boring hour. He couldn't even visualize the kind of a service filled with joy and praise that his son was so enthused about.

In a Touch of Beauty Bible Study one day, we dug into the Scriptures for information about our children and church attendance. It was an interesting time, because we represented many different backgrounds and churches. There were Catholic mothers, Baptist mothers and Lutherans, and a lot of others whose denominations I could only guess.

Mind Your Manner!

We began with Hebrews 10:25, which says, "Not forsaking the assembling of yourselves together, *as the manner of some is*; but exhorting one another: and so much the more, as ye see the day approaching." There you have the commandment which has caused Christians through the ages to believe in the necessity of regular church attendance. Even in the early church, there were apparently a few who felt they didn't need the church or Christian fellowship. They had this manner—this habit—which came from the attitude, "I can make it on my own, just Jesus and me. After all, it's not going to church that makes you a Christian; it's being born again!" Yes, and the Bible also says, "By this shall all men know that ye are my disciples, if ye have love one to another" (John 13:35); and, "We know that we have passed from death unto life, because we love the brethren" (1 John 3:14).

It's a brash contradiction to say you know Jesus but do not love His people. To claim to be a part of the Body of Christ yet live life independently of that Body doesn't make a bit of sense to me. It's as if one of your hands suddenly declared its independence and marched over to stand alone in the corner because it didn't care for the behavior of your shoulder! But the really serious damage done by Christians like this is the damage to their children. Those children are taught *about* Christ, *about* the Bible. But their parents' example teaches them most fluently that the Body of Christ is not important, that ministering to brothers and sisters in the family and receiving their ministry is not important; and worshipping God is just something you do when you feel in the mood. These children are deprived of the beautiful ministry operated through the gifts of the Spirit in a local church for the edifying of the Body. They miss the blessings of close fellowship and of having a force of faith to draw upon in times of emergency.

Jesus showed us by His example that, while going to worship services regularly is not salvation, it is important. He was faithful in His attendance at the synagogue every Sabbath, even though He was the Son of God. We don't teach a child to go to church because it impresses God or gets him to heaven. We teach him to go to worship the Lord because He is worthy. We teach him also to minister to others. If your children are small, you might wish to get them involved in the children's worship services for their age group. In our congregation, we have services for two- and three-year-olds, four- and five-year-olds, and first through third graders. In each service, the children learn to worship in a way meaningful to them. A second grader has the privilege of doing much more on Sunday than observing adults worship. He's in a church where his friends worship and pray with him. He gets to share his answers to prayer. He hears a sermon that's presented at his age level.

Using Your Tools

Perhaps it's become obvious to you that again we're talking about our set of Parents' Training Tools—example, encouragement, explanation, experience and correction. These are always involved in our parenting, no matter what subject we're discussing, but they're especially crucial when we focus on habits and attitudes. Here's how I see them applying to my own efforts:

Explanation: It's good to teach verses that make a positive confession about worship and praising God. For instance, Psalm 57:7, "My heart is fixed on God: I will sing and give praise." That's an attitude that I call a worshipful spirit, and it's coupled with the habit of thankfulness.

Correction: If we want that attitude of thankfulness and habit of worship, then two things we must continually correct are negativism and complaining. Children are vulnerable to both those habits. (We adults are not, of course!) And adolescents are *especially* vulnerable (in case you haven't noticed)! A thankful spirit will never develop in a negative environment. Our children can go to church every Sunday, yet never become worshipful people because we allow them to spend the other six days of the week complaining and giving glory to the devil for all his despicable work.

Example: If your child sees that you look forward to going to church, enjoy the services, and love your pastor and the people in the church, he will pick up that same spirit.

Encouragement: Commend your children for their attentiveness to the sermon and their participation in the singing. Don't give them attention only when they misbehave or when they drop the songbook with a crash! Perhaps some of the deliberate efforts of a pastor's wife may be of use to you:

When our first child was born, I knew she faced a life filled with church-going—not only regular services, but also youth camps, conferences, and the many outside places where my husband preaches. I didn't want to always leave her with a baby-sitter, so we determined that going to church would be a pleasant experience. It's hard to say which of my attempts were successful —but something—or a combination of somethings—did work. When the girls reached school age, I'd occasionally get a sitter for them during an evening service, and you'd think I'd just grounded them for a week! It was worse than punishment to be made to stay home from a service! And our services are not short! My husband feels that sermonettes make Christianettes. So he preaches forty-five minutes, sometimes an hour. At eight, Carmen visited another church with her Brownie Troop. Her comment was that it was a good service, but the sermon was awfully short!

I think I can honestly say that both of the older girls enjoy church. They never ask to stay home! (Jamie, of course, is ecstatic at the mention of it—wants to go every day to play with his two-year-old girl friends, Amber and Crystal!)

Healthy youth groups, loving teachers, dedicated children's church leaders—all have been most responsible for this, but I also have to think about the many hours they've spent in services planned for the whole family. We've never approached them with the feeling that a child is there to learn to sit still. My children are there to worship, learn, participate and be kept interested. If they get restless listening to the sermon, I hand out a picture book or paper and colors. When they reach first grade or begin to read, I help them look up the scriptures and point to the words as the pastor reads. Our girls have colored myriads of pictures in church, but after a while, it became obvious they were absorbing great amounts of the Word as they colored.

Sitting in church is a good time for affection, for cuddling and loving. When our congregation was smaller and there were no nurseries for four- and five-year-olds, it was a usual thing for Christi to spend the whole sermon being hugged and patted in mother's arms, falling asleep with her head on my shoulder. It seems inevitable that she will always think of church and the presence of God as a place of comfort, love and warmth. Besides, what's more pleasurable for a mother? I had the double delight of good preaching and the quiet cuddling there never seems to be time enough for at home!

Children too old to cuddle find pleasure in the singing, in special music groups, in the sacraments of the church. For the last few years, Christi and her friends always want to sit close to the baptistry on Sunday nights and Thursday nights—they want to be in the dead center of the excitement of each one who declares his new life there.

In Matthew 21 we can read about children praising Jesus in the temple. And He accepted their praise. It was valid. It was just as precious to God as the praise of adults. Children of today will praise Jesus if they're given half a chance—and if we don't insist they do it in the ways adults do. Give your child that chance—expose him every Sunday to the kind of worship that uplifts Jesus, praises Jesus—authentically and meaningfully.

Fellowship: The Purifying Addiction

Closely connected to all this is the habit of *Christian fellowship.* As adult Christians, we understand the value of Christian fellowship for ourselves, but have you ever thought of the implications of Christian fellowship for children? If Christian fellowship strengthens your relationship with Christ, encourages you and ministers to your needs, then it will also do that for your four-year-old boy or your nine-year-old girl.

Here are promises about fellowship from 1 John 1, "That which we have seen and heard declare we unto you, that ye also may have fellowship with us: and truly our fellowship is with the Father, and with his Son Jesus Christ.... If we walk in the light, as he is in the light, we have fellowship one with another, and the blood of Jesus Christ his Son cleanseth us from all sin" (vv. 3, 7).

Christian fellowship is a purifying experience. As we fellowship with one another, a sterilizing process goes on in our lives. I don't know exactly how it works, but God has designed this to keep us free from the dust of the world that accumulates on us. As we fellowship with brothers and sisters in Christ, the blood of Christ is continually cleansing us and keeping us clean and righteous. But do you see, then, what happens if we neglect to fellowship with other Christians? We begin to soak in the corruption which is part of this world; it piles up, invades our thinking, and we grow dusty and lukewarm in our love for Christ. That's why it's so important for us as parents and for our children to see that fellowship is a regular, habitual part of our lives, not just something we do when we get to feeling terribly low, or when there's a special program at the church, or when we have a new dress to show off!

We must teach children by our example that Christian fellowship is something we do as consistently as we make the beds and cook the meals. We're Christians, therefore we fellowship with other Christians—not because the preacher puts pressure on us to be in services; and not because we expect a boost to our ego and self-importance when we work in the church. We teach children by our fellowship that it's valuable, enjoyable, strengthening, purifying, and commanded by the Word. I'm not talking here only about the fellowship involved in church services, but also about fellowship with children of their own age who know Jesus, about Christian friendships, youth activities, camps and fun times.

Evaluate Your Example!

Evaluate your own fellowship and see if it's an attractive example to your child. When he sees you get together with another Christian couple, does he see the love of Christ expressed in your relationship? As he watches you relate to the people at church, what does he learn about your attitudes toward them? Does he see that you genuinely love and enjoy them?

One day I was having a delightful conversation on the phone with a Christian friend. She was sharing how the Lord had so miraculously healed her just that week, and we were praising God together. Then we got carried away just visiting, laughing and joking. After I'd hung up, my six-year-old asked, "Mommy, why did you talk so long to her?" "Well, because I wanted to," I said. "Susan is my friend and I really love her. We have a good time just talking." That's a small thing, but I wanted to convey to my child that Christian fellowship is a pleasant thing, and if she heard any of the conversation, she caught that feeling.

It's good to explain Christian fellowship to a child in terms that are understandable to him. For example, let's say Jimmy asks the question, "Why do we go to church so much, Mommy?" Your explanation will leave an indelible impression in his mind. Be careful what you say! One thing you could say is, "We like to go to church. We like to be with our Christian friends, and we enjoy worshipping the Lord together." I've found that kind of an answer creates a certain feeling in my children, and as they've grown it's become their attitude. They look forward to Sunday because they have developed close friendships with many children their own ages. We must not underrate the fellowship children have with each other.

How to Encourage?

Unfortunately, as great as fellowship is for children, it's a habit that will not stick without encouragement. There will be days when they don't feel like going to Sunday school. There are emotional ups and downs that can keep them away from Christian friends. And there are those awkward self-conscious stages that adolescent girls go through where they'll sit home every night of the week rather than face their peers. Teenage girls will skip the youth group because a pimple appears, and fourth grade girls will miss a Christmas party because they squabbled with another girl in the group. When our daughter was three, she came home from Sunday school very slighted one day. "Mommy," she said, "not one person complimented my new shoes!" Well, it's at these times your encouragement is so important. If you understand the value of regular fellowship, you will see to it that little trifles don't interrupt it.

A friend shared with me her childhood experiences in a youth camp. Even now, as a mother of five, Jodi tends to be quiet and somewhat shy, but she's a capable wife and mother, as well as a dedicated Christian. As a child, she was so shy, she hardly ever spoke to a soul. When her parents informed her she was being sent to the church youth camp, it seemed like the most horrible thing that could happen. She was miserable that whole week, but toward the end she began to make a few friends and gained a little confidence. The next year, her parents forced her to camp again, but this time it was a little easier; and it became easier each year, as she went every single summer through junior high and high school. Jodi now looks back on those camping experiences as the single most valuable part of her growing up. "It was there," she said, "I really learned to know Christ; and because of the fellowship with kids my own age who were loving Him, I learned to love Him." Jodi's parents may have seemed cruel to their onlooking friends, but what they were really doing was encouraging the development of the habit of Christian fellowship.

A wise mother will encourage Christian fellowship by keeping her home open to kids from Christian groups. If there's a child your girl likes at Sunday school, make it a point to invite her home for dinner. Plan some outings or dinners with Christian families who have children. In the days we're living in, it's best to have an overbalance of Christian friends for your child. He'll meet plenty of the other kind at school, so make sure you counteract that influence with a large and active bunch of kids who love the Lord. A child *will* have a social life. He'll find a way, because it's natural for him to want to be a part of a group. If you don't provide a Christian gang for him to fellowship in, it's likely he will seek out another kind of gang. I know it's extra trouble: it's usually inconvenient—a child's friends can even drive you out of your mind with giggles and silliness; but if you understand the benefits, you'll make the effort.

Families in our church often "trade children" for a few days. Mary and Leila both have girls near the same age and boys near the same age. To make a fun weekend for the kids, Mary will trade her boy for Leila's girl. The two girls have a good time staying overnight and giggling, while the two boys climb trees. Strong and wholesome friendships are built with no undue strain on either mother.

Concerned Correction

Another time, Marty worried about her adolescent daughter who was beginning to choose friends at school that were a little questionable. It was nice weather, so Marty invited about five boys and five girls from the church, packed a picnic lunch and a softball, and headed for Blue Lake Park. For herself, she took a blanket and a stack of books. That way she could let the kids stay as long as they liked—which turned out to be all day! During that day, the Christian fellowship had a chance to really develop, and those kids found out they really liked being together. One thing led to another, and the undesirable friends at school faded out of the picture. Now, that's a subtle form of correction. But, some kind of correction is always needed whenever you see a child neglecting Christian fellowship or becoming overbalanced in his friendships.

When a child withdraws into a shell and refuses to associate with others in his youth group, check carefully before you ignore it or blame it on others. A little correction may straighten out the problem. Do it gently and with wisdom, but don't stand by and let shyness or inhibition keep your son or daughter from this ingredient of a strong Christian life.

Attitudes Are Delicate!

When it comes to building attitudes, I can't think of a single area more delicate than this one of fellowship. For instance, you can send a child to Sunday school regularly, building the *habit* of fellowship; but if you are not going with him, the *attitude* he picks up is that Sunday school and Bible study are things children do, but not adults. If he hears his Sunday school teacher or superintendent criticized at home, the subtle *attitude* creeps in which says all Christians are just phonies after all. There are dozens of spiritual dropouts lying around who were taught good habits of fellowship but a wrong attitude—kids who were allowed to condemn and criticize their peers in the Body of Christ or to quit Sunday school because they didn't like the teacher. They failed to learn that important spirit of love and respect for the Body of Christ.

Don't permit a child to make fun of a slow child in his children's church. Don't allow him to run down a friend or an enemy. Teach him the concepts of Romans 12, which talks about honoring one another, loving each other fervently. Love and criticism cannot coexist. To allow one is to negate the other.

It's so sad to see adults poisoning the mind of a child towards the church by careless remarks and eating "roast preacher" for dinner. If you're unhappy with your church, don't talk about it in front of your children—please don't! It could be that the problem is you, not the church. Why not become part of the solution, rather than part of the problem? It's amazing how quickly some Christians begin to grow in a church after their attitude is changed from negative to positive. Be discreet in the way you talk about individual Christians in the church—even your closest friends and relatives! A child may not appear to be listening, but he's absorbing a lot more than meets the eye.

Hypocrites in the Church?

How often do you meet adults who are turned off to Christianity because of hypocrites in the church and people who claim they grew up in the church but saw so much hypocrisy in the lives of adults. I have a sneaking suspicion that a lot of these casualties came not because those children actually saw Christians living double lives but because of what they heard in their homes. Listening to Mom and Dad talk about the faults of Sister Smith, the children got the impression Sister Smith was not anything like she appeared in church. Evidently she was just pretending all that time. You see, a child's mind doesn't distinguish between immaturity and phoniness. He doesn't realize there are people of all growth levels in a group of Christians. So he comes to inaccurate conclusions about people as he takes in adult conversation.

One Sunday night a man visited our church with his wife, who was being baptized. As I greeted him, he said something like this, "I don't know what this church has done for my wife, but I'm here to find out. She's sure been a different person lately." Then he went on to explain how he had rejected church after church because in each he had found hypocrites. I just *had* to answer that, so I said, "Well, Don, I don't know a lot of the people here tonight, but I suppose some of them are hypocrites, too. And I hope they keep coming. We've seen an awfully lot of hypocrites come to Christ and have their lives transformed into the real thing. I don't know of a better place for a hypocrite to come, do you?" Don came back again—and again—to the church. One night he came to the conclusion that the real hypocrites were to be found in the bar, laughing it up and pretending happiness—those men who were so empty on the inside. He exchanged his own hypocritical life for a real one—in Jesus.

I'd like to start a campaign to get adults to quit poisoning the minds of children against the church. Would you help me?

Today, why don't you pray this prayer about the conversation you hold in the presence of a child, "Let the words of my mouth, and the meditation of my heart, be acceptable in thy sight, O Lord, my strength, and my redeemer" (Ps. 19:14). Let your children grow up with a healthy attitude of love and respect for the Body of Christ. The fellowship habits we build will then lead him into two more attitudes that will determine his entire future:

1. The desire to do God's will.
2. The desire for a Christian marriage and home.

Desire to Do God's Will

Two verses key all our teaching of Christian living and attitudes:

> I delight to do thy will, O my God: yea, thy law is within my heart (Ps. 40:8).

> For this is the love of God, that we keep his commandments: and his commandments are not grievous (1 John 5:3).

If children are to desire God's will—His plans for their lives—they need to be convinced it's the happiest way to live, that doing His will is a delight, a pleasure, not a hard, grievous, painful way of life. That attitude is not necessarily learned in a Christian home. It is only learned in a *happy* Christian home where parents are actually experiencing the truth that true pleasure comes in living the way we were built to live—for Jesus. Mothers who behave like self-styled martyrs, "carrying the cross," are living a repulsive picture of the Christian life. This is phony! It's a lie! The Bible says the way of the *sinner* is hard! (Not the way of the Christian!) Jesus said His yoke was easy and His burden light! It's living for the devil that's tough—not living for Jesus! This concept will flow from our mouths and actions in every habit we teach—it will be the unspoken effect of our life-styles on our kids. If we convince them that doing God's will is going to be whatever you hate, wherever you don't want to go, because this cruel God is out to take away everything you enjoy and give you a life of suffering—then our children will not *desire* to do God's will. When they leave our homes, they'll make career decisions, marriage decisions—all those life-shaping choices—without acknowledging God and without seeking His guidance. That's frightening! In all our training of habits and attitudes, the experience of living with happy parents is most essential.

The Desire for a Christian Home

Have you thought about your child and the home he will some day build, about the man or woman he will marry and the grandchildren you will enjoy? For young mothers, that probably seems very remote; but I know that if you have a teenager in the home, you're beginning to consider such things. If you're a woman who loves the Lord, there's one thing I know you want for your child's future—a Christian marriage and a Christian home. Have you given the child this same desire? Not all children who grow up in godly homes desire to establish one of their own. It's not an automatic tendency they inherit, like blue eyes or curly hair! That desire is another of those attitudes we place deep inside a child by our training.

If the habit of fellowship is built, then part of your training for a Christian marriage is already done. If your boy grows up with many friends who love Christ and enjoy a rich social life, it's likely he will choose his mate from among Christian people. I'm not talking about denominations now. The issue is not one of marrying outside your church; the issue is marrying an unbeliever, a person who has never accepted Christ as Saviour, never been born into the Kingdom of God. That's why we begin early to teach our children 2 Corinthians 6:14-16: "Be ye not unequally yoked together with unbelievers: for what fellowship hath righteousness with unrighteousness? and what communion hath light with darkness? And what concord hath Christ with Belial? or what part hath he that believeth with an infidel? And what agreement hath the temple of God with idols? for ye are the temple of the living God; as God hath said, I will dwell in them, and walk in them; and I will be their God, and they shall be my people."

One of my good friends had a loving and wise father in her teenage years. She was a pretty girl and had many opportunities to date; but with each request the father would ask, "Is he a Christian?" Melva might say, "He's a real nice guy, Dad. He goes to church." "That's not what I asked. Is he born again? Is he a Christian?" "Well, he's never said so." Then the father would open his Bible to this passage (2 Cor. 6:14) and ask the daughter to read it aloud. "I'm sorry, honey, but I can't disobey God and let you go out with this boy, even though I am sure he's very nice and good looking." After graduation from high school, Melva met a young businessman who determined he would take her out. He went to her father's home to persuade the stubborn man. The father immediately asked him, "Son, are you a born-again Christian? Do you know Christ as your Saviour?" The businessman looked uncertain, and the father began to explain to him why he was reluctant to let his daughter go. Then he began witnessing to the poor fellow. Melva fled to her room in tears. "I'll never see him again!" she thought as she listened to her father preach at least an hour. The young man left the house, unsuccessful in changing her father's mind. But as he drove down the road, that strong man found himself crying. Finally, he had to stop his car—he couldn't see to drive! Don Koch accepted Jesus into his life that night, then grew into a strong Christian and married Melva. The man who protected his daughter so stubbornly was blessed with a Christian son-in-law and six grandchildren who love Jesus.

Henry Hill, Patriarch

The name of this wise father was Henry Hill, a man who is now with the Lord, but highly revered in the minds of us who knew him. Even the memory of his life inspires fathers and mothers today because Henry truly understood the eternal value of his children. Money was not the priority in his life. His job was not the priority, nor the material things the job could provide. He raised his family on a farm near a small town called Boring, Oregon. But life on that farm was far from boring—it was alive with Christian fellowship.

Henry and Melvina were determined their children would grow up to serve Jesus and establish Christian homes of their own. To reach that goal, no sacrifice was spared—no price was too great. The best fellowship and most excitement in Oregon of the fifties was in Portland—first in the history-making Billy Graham Crusades of 1950, and then in the Portland Youth for Christ rallies.

Melva sang in the choir for that crusade, and the entire family was there every night. It was nearly a sixty-minute trip from Boring to Portland in Henry's '37 Ford, but the Hills felt the worth of that experience to their teenage children was more valuable than their tiredness, the gas, travel time or lost sleep.

Henry worked at the Union Depot in Portland and often had to work on Saturdays. But that didn't discourage him from getting the kids to Saturday night Y.F.C. He'd drive home from work, pile the teens in his Ford and head back to Portland, sometimes on an empty stomach—there had been no time for supper!

Henry Hill personally led each of his children to Jesus at home. Then he gave them the support of family Bible study and prayer. When they became teens, he knew their very lives depended on the quality of fellowship they received. Money was not plenteous, but he made it stretch when Melva wanted to go to Wheaton for the National YFC Conference. And he found a way to provide a social life for the whole family that revolved around loving, laughing, wholesome fellowship. It is no accident that his children grew up with a desire to do God's will and a desire for Christian homes like the one they'd experienced. Here's a man who was successful for eternity. I'm just selfish enough to want the same kind of success—whatever the cost!

Have Your Own Bible Study

Habits and Attitudes for Healthy Christians

1. Bible Study: 1 Pet. 2:2; Ps. 119:16, 24, 47, 97, 103 (love and enjoyment of God's Word).
2. Church attendance, worship and fellowship: Neh. 12:43; Heb. 10:25; John 13:35; 1 John 3:14; Ps. 57:7; Matt. 21:15-16; 1 John 1:3, 7; Ps. 19:14; Rom. 12 (patterns of loving fellowship).
3. The desire to do God's will and the desire to have a Christian home: Ps. 40:8; 1 John 5:3; Matt. 11:28-30; 2 Cor. 6:14-16.

Chapter 9

Children, Money and God

One of the most helpful habits you can train in a child is the habit of tithing. Christian families have long been aware that there's a direct correlation between tithing and prosperity. The Bible says so, and it really does work out that way. But when and how do we go about teaching this principle to our children? Is it too much to expect a child to part with his few pennies when he's small? Will he resent a God whom he can't see, yet must give his money to? These are interesting questions, and we need to find answers to them in Scripture. If God tells the truth, then His promises are just as true for a child as they are for an adult. At a very early age, a child can begin learning to trust and worship God at every level of his life. What we teach a child about money and giving influences his future attitudes, whether materialistic and covetous or heavenly minded and generous. If we teach him to honor God with his money, trust Him with the needs of his life, we won't have to worry about his prosperity as an adult.

God has promised to bless every person, child or adult, who honors Him with his money. The commandment to tithe is found in Malachi 3:10. I don't think this verse is too complicated for a child of five or six to comprehend: "Bring ye all the tithes into the storehouse, that there may be meat in mine house, and prove me now herewith, saith the Lord of hosts, if I will not open you the windows of heaven, and pour you out a blessing, that there shall not be room enough to receive it. And I will rebuke the devourer for your sakes, and he shall not destroy the fruits of your ground; neither shall your vine cast her fruit before the time in the field, saith the Lord of hosts." In explaining this to a child, simply state that when we give God a full tenth of our income, we can expect Him to pour abundant prosperity upon us. We will not suffer poverty because we have given God His portion of money; instead, we will have such plenty it will be overwhelming.

Carmen became a believer in giving at age eight. She came home from children's church one Sunday, explaining that they had decided to take an offering in their service. "And, Mommy, we're going to give our own money. We don't want our parents to give us change for this offering." "Fine," I said, "a good idea." On Sunday, she went to her piggy bank and counted her savings. I wasn't giving allowances at that time, so her income was limited to nickels she'd earned doing odd jobs, or dimes Daddy had given her. She'd accumulated 47¢. I was shocked when she emptied the *whole* piggy bank into her purse. "Are you sure you want to put *all* your money in the offering?" "Yes, Mom, I want to give the whole thing!" I didn't want to discourage a spirit like that, so I just prayed the Lord would reward her.

For several days that child was penniless. Then a letter came in the mail, addressed to Carmen Cook. In it was a check for the largest amount of money she'd ever seen—$20.00. Months before, Grandpa had taken her beat-up old bicycle and fixed it, hoping to sell it for her. A day or so after she put her money in the offering, a buyer "happened" to come along; and here was so much money she could hardly decide how to spend it. The first thing she did was to pay $2.00 tithe! But that's not the end! While she was deciding how to spend the $18.00, God poured out more. She was wondering whether to buy a swimming pool or a big red wagon. Meanwhile, one of my friends called: "We're moving, and I have some things to give Carmen and Christi." Well, that was quite a day. They came home with a great big wagon, a red pedal car, a beautiful doll house with ten rooms of furniture and all kinds of smaller toys. It was a child's dream come true! Then Carmen bought her "swimming pool" and still had $5.00 left. The children had a summer packed full of fun with all their new toys. Carmen learned that you never out-give God. She gave Him 47¢, and He gave back $20.00, plus all the toys her heart could desire!

When your child voluntarily begins to tithe and give offerings in church, you can be sure some spiritual growth is taking place. At that point, what you encourage or correct can be very decisive. Your example is going to come under some scrutiny. The way in which you give money to the Lord's work will be noticeable to the child. Does he see you give it generously and joyfully because you love the Lord, or does he catch a begrudging, stingy spirit that says you're giving because it's a Christian duty? One idea is that a good example involves putting something in the offering each time it's taken in the church and letting the child put something in, even if it's just a dime. A habit is being built, one that will last a lifetime and help a child to put God first in his life.

As the habit of Bible study trains respect and love for the Word of God, so the habit of giving trains love for God and a pattern of putting Him first. It's good for a child to express his love for God in a tangible way. It helps his love to grow. The pennies he gives may not seem like much to you, but then how do you place a price value on the bouquet of dandelions he brings you? When a gift expresses love, it's valuable to both the receiver and the giver. That's part of what Jesus was talking about in the incident of the widow's mite. He saw the great love in a woman's heart and counted it more valuable than the wealth of the rich man who gave without love. (By the way, that widow didn't go away and starve because she gave her last penny to God! My Father takes care of His children. He's promised to supply all our needs.) "Give," He said, "and it shall be given unto you, good measure, pressed down and running over." That promise is dependable for you and for your children, no matter how small they are. The sooner they begin experiencing the truth of that promise, the better. They'll never waste energy worrying about money if they've had a taste of the abundant provision of God all through their childhood.

When Christi was five, she saved her money all summer to go to Disneyland. At the same time, she wanted a bicycle badly. Every other child on the street had a bike, and all day long they rode up and down the street, leaving her with no choice but to run along behind or sit home alone. She prayed to Jesus for a bike, and two concerned parents were trying to find a way to afford one. In August we took the trip to California, and in her purse Christi had carefully secured $10.50 in change, enough to enter Disneyland and buy a few treats. First we went for a week to a youth camp where my husband was the speaker. One night Christi took her purse with her to the big chapel and accidentally left it there. We returned to search for it, but a sick feeling hit me as I realized it had been stolen, maybe by one of the sinners my husband was trying to reach! There was nothing to do but return to our cabin and pray that Jesus would help us get it back. The children prayed very specifically—for the purse *and* the $10.50. They were confident we'd get both, and said no more about it. But I was a little worried about their faith! Nothing happened until the last *hour* of camp. Then the Camp Director announced to the five hundred teenagers that Christi had lost her purse. Had any of them seen it? The response of those kids was to grab a big empty can and run through the crowd collecting change to replace her money. As the campers were leaving Cedarcrest, two teenagers counted it out for Christi. In that can was $44.00 in dimes and quarters! Then, a few hours later, her lost pure showed up in the camp office, with the money intact. The thief had given in to a guilty conscience!

Needless to say, the Christian love those kids showed a five-year-old girl really made an impression on her life; but the extra $44.00, she knew, was the answer to her prayer for a bike. After a wonderful time at Disneyland, she had the privilege of riding her answer to prayer down the street alongside all her little friends. The blessings of Jesus never cease to overwhelm me.

His kindness to my children extends to every part of their lives—whether it's money, health, food or clothing. I learned He does care about their finances just as He cares about mine.

What you teach your child about money will drastically shape his whole life. Have you ever thought of that? How we relate to money reveals some of the deepest traits of our character. Our daily responses to financial needs can show we have faith in God, or a lack of trust. Our handling of money shows whether we are basically selfish or unselfish, covetous or content. We pass on to our children our attitude towards money, and with that attitude a multitude of others which will determine whether their lives are lived for materialistic purposes or godly purposes. Most of our training in handling money centers upon thrift, good management, saving and the like. If we're not careful, we breed an attitude that money is the most precious commodity of life, and one that's to be used for "me only"! We try to teach children the value of money by giving them some to handle. We encourage them to save towards something.

But what if a child wants to dip into his savings and give a dime to his chum at school, uses some of it to help little sister buy a new dolly, or, suppose your child is really challenged by a missionary who speaks at church and shows slides of needy people in far-off Africa? Should a child be allowed to give money at a time when he's emotionally stirred? What is your reaction?

These are the kinds of small incidents that can tell you a lot about yourself, as a person and as a Christian. To get a perspective on how you measure up to Scripture, think about verses like these: "It is possible to give away and become richer! It is also possible to hold on too tightly and lose everything. Yes, the liberal man shall be rich! By watering others, he waters himself." (That's Proverbs 11:24 and 25 from the Living Bible.) It's a good rule of thumb to guide you in handling your own money and in training a child. Proverbs 19:17, "When you help the poor you are lending to the Lord and He pays wonderful interest on your loan."

Proverbs 28:27, "If you give to the poor, your needs will be supplied! But a curse upon those who close their eyes to poverty. Greed causes fighting: trusting God leads to prosperity." Matthew 6:33, "Seek ye first the Kingdom of God and His righteousness and all these things shall be added unto you."

I think it's obvious that we should teach a child generosity and compassion with His money, right along with thrift and diligence. If we teach him the concepts that are found in the Word of God, we can then relax and let God prove to the child himself that His promises really are true. So don't ever discourage a giving spirit in a child. Remember, he is basically a self-centered and selfish person to begin with! Any move in the opposite direction should be welcomed! If he loves God or any human being enough to part with some of his pennies, that's a good indication he's transferring some interest away from himself and on to others.

Now there's another concept regarding money that children should grow up with. It's also found in the Bible, and it's the concept that money is something you must work to get. In our affluent society we have many kids growing up thinking the world owes them a living. They criticize the materialism of their parents, but turn to those same parents for money when their welfare check runs out. A child needs to have opportunities to *earn* money so that he can understand that money is something given in exchange for part of his time and energy. It's good to give allowances, but we should make them small enough to make extra work a necessity to earn the luxuries for which children yearn. Scripture is clear on the relationship of work to money: "For even when we were with you, this we commanded you, that if any would not work, neither should he eat" (2 Thess. 3:10). Proverbs 13:4, "Lazy people want much but get little, while the diligent are prospering." Proverbs 14:23, "Work brings profit: talk brings poverty!" That's putting it pretty bluntly! So does this one, "If you won't plow in the cold you won't eat at the harvest" (Prov. 20:4). Don't give your child much money. Let him learn the value of money by working for it. Twenty years from now you'll be glad you did, because it's a scriptural principle which governs our lives on this earth.

There are also Bible principles concerning prosperity and good management which you can teach a child in your training about money. The Bible lists nine or ten good keys to prosperity. Some of them are generosity, tithing and giving, hard work, diligence, resourcefulness, wise spending and planning ahead. For a complete study of biblical principles of money management, I strongly recommend Malcolm MacGregor's book entitled *Your Money Matters*,* which is a practical, down-to-earth guide for a Christian family. Also your church or city may sponsor his Financial Seminar for Family Living—if so, by all means attend that and learn to live without financial distress.

I'd like to make a few practical suggestions about allowances, children's spending, and earnings. Mothers often ask, "Should I give my child an allowance, or should I pay him for working around the house?" The problem with paying a child for the tasks he does at home, of course, is that he becomes mercenary, demanding a nickel for every tiny thing you ask him to do. And we feel that as a member of a family who's sharing the house, the food, the pleasures of a warm bed and good care, each child should willingly carry his share of the work. So most of us would be reluctant to pay children for every small job, or for daily duties like taking out the garbage or setting the table. We're afraid of building selfishness, among other negatives. You have the same problem when you give a weekly allowance in exchange for doing set duties around the house. It's still pay for something you really know he should do without pay. If confronted with a request from Mother to help with dinner, the child can come back with, "That's not one of the jobs I have to do for my allowance!" On the other hand, simply giving a child a weekly allowance eliminates the training that money is something you must work to get, teaching that money is something other people should give to

---

*Published by Bethany Fellowship, Inc., 1977.

you. I feel the solution to this is (1) a small allowance, (2) regular household chores that are done without pay, and (3) opportunities provided to earn extra money when a child wants something special. Using this guideline, in our home we start with a weekly allowance of 50¢ ($1.00 for an older child). We give it in small change, so that a child can easily pick a nickel out of it for tithe every Sunday. Anything beyond that nickel they can also take to Sunday school (if they wish), but that one nickel out of each 50¢ they learn is God's money.

A small allowance gives a child a little spending money for an occasional candy bar, coloring book, or he can save it for something big. But when our children get a yearning for a big toy, they've learned they must work to earn the money for it. After the daily jobs are finished, they can ask for extra jobs to earn quarters. A list of typical "quarter" jobs would look something like this: "Wash the bedroom walls, clean up the yard, scrub the kitchen floor, vacuum the furniture, polish the mirrors."

At six and eight, the girls decided they wanted a Barbie's Country Camper. They counted their money and, by pooling it, came up with $4.25. We went to the store and found a country camper for $9.96. They laid it away and went home with a tremendous motivation to work for the remaining dollars. For a couple of weeks, it kept me busy thinking up enough jobs for them to do (it is helpful to keep a written list of jobs for children), but it was a proud day when they finally were able to bring home the wonderful toy. That camper became the favorite toy. Along with the joy it gave them, it taught them some very scriptural concepts about work and money. They learned you can have what you want if you're willing to work hard. They also learned that you must honor God with your money if you want His blessing. It could have been a temptation to save the tithe money to help pay for the camper; but neither child would permit the other to do that!

In our teaching about money, let's teach children about life. Let's teach them the joys of achieving a goal, earning, and saving. And let's build habits to help a child live unselfishly and with God truly in first place.

Have Your Own Bible Study

Children, Money and God

1. Tithing: Mal. 3:8-10.
2. Promises about giving, generosity, and God's provision for us: Luke 21:1-4; Phil. 4:19; Luke 6:38; Prov. 11:24-25; 19:17; 28:27; Matt. 6:33.
3. Work: 2 Thess. 3:10; Prov. 13:4; 14:23; 20:4.

SECTION 3

Training Your Child for Living

Chapter 10

Children's Fears

Today's children make up one of the most anxiety ridden generations yet to live on this earth. They're constantly exposed to powerful influences that implant fear. All the tragedies of the world are brought before their innocent eyes on television; a daily diet of the 6 o'clock news in living color would be enough to turn a normal nine-year-old into a neurotic! No wonder we've seen an increase of mental illness in teenagers! Because of an increased knowledge of world events—things like torture in Africa, persecution in Viet Nam, and airline crashes in the U.S.—children are more aware of the existing dangers that threaten them. Gone are the days when a child could live in blissful ignorance of evil, of crime, rape and earthquakes, simply because they never touched his village.

The question is, How do Christian mothers deal with children's fears in today's world, both the imaginary fears and the real ones? We realize that a certain amount of fear is both normal and healthy; we *need* to be afraid in a truly dangerous situation—afraid enough to generate the energy and speed to escape it. We want our boy to fear fire; enough so that he will not play with matches, but not so much that he lies awake nights wondering if his house is on fire. We teach a child to be afraid of a stranger who tries to get him into a car. But when a fourth grader is afraid to walk to school because of imaginary kidnappers, that's abnormal fear.

All children have experiences at one time or another that cause them fear: being in a car accident, getting lost in a big store, falling into a river, or *almost* getting hit by a car. The way we as parents deal with these events can make our children well adjusted or neurotic —it really depends on us!

Factual Basis for Fearless Living

I believe children can live lives free from unhealthy fears if their parents believe and teach them the Word of God. That, combined with a secure, loving family, is the greatest preventative of and cure for anxiety. The Bible is filled with promises for physical protection —promises a Christian mother can claim for her child. When you know and use these promises, you'll not need to be an over-protective mother. The problem is, many parents do not know what they can ask for. And James 4:2 flatly says, "Ye have not, because ye ask not." When we live in ignorance of the promises of God, we live in uncertainty, never knowing what the future holds, always a little fearful that some tragedy may come along.

There are hundreds of promises for protection to the godly in the Bible—protection from murderers, rapists, burglars; protection in the middle of natural disasters like floods and earthquakes or famines and war. Mother, do you know these promises? Could you fight a spiritual battle with these weapons in an emergency? We've used them in the face of certain death for two of our children. Christian mothers have been awakened to use them in the night for a son on the front lines of a battlefield, later to find that a miracle had occurred to save the son, right at the time that mother was praying, claiming those promises! At the end of this chapter, you'll find a short list of some of the promises for protection; learn at least those, if you haven't already, and teach them to your children. But the best place to start is in Psalm 91. Read it now with your child in mind; it gives a factual, intelligent basis for fearless living:

> He that dwelleth in the secret place of the most High shall abide under the shadow of the Almighty.
> I will say of the Lord, He is my refuge and my fortress: my God; in him will I trust.

Surely he shall deliver thee from the snare of the fowler, and from the noisome pestilence.

He shall cover thee with his feathers, and under his wings shalt thou trust: his truth shall be thy shield and buckler.

Thou shalt not be afraid for the terror by night; nor for the arrow that flieth by day;

Nor for the pestilence that walketh in darkness; nor for the destruction that wasteth at noonday.

A thousand shall fall at thy side, and ten thousand at thy right hand; but it shall not come nigh thee.

Only with thine eyes shalt thou behold and see the reward of the wicked.

Because thou hast made the Lord, which is my refuge, even the most High, thy habitation;

There shall no evil befall thee, neither shall any plague come nigh thy dwelling.

For he shall give his angels charge over thee, to keep thee in all thy ways.

They shall bear thee up in their hands, lest thou dash thy foot against a stone.

Thou shalt tread upon the lion and adder: the young lion and the dragon shalt thou trample under feet.

Because he hath set his love upon me, therefore will I deliver him: I will set him on high, because he hath known my name.

He shall call upon me, and I will answer him: I will be with him in trouble; I will deliver him, and honour him.

With long life will I satisfy him, and show him my salvation.

Don't you think that reads like a too-good-to-be-real insurance policy? It offers protection from plagues, epidemics, protection from Satan (and even power over him), protection in times of war, even safety for a Christian flying on an airplane! (vv. 11, 12). In fact, it goes so far as to say, if you can believe it and live close to God, "there shall *no evil* befall thee!" That's heavy! These promises are not, of course, to the whole human race; they're to the committed people of God (vv. 1, 2, 14), who will use them and learn to call upon God with faith in an emergency, rather than panic and fear (vv. 14, 15, 16). When you can develop that attitude of security, you have the basis for raising children who will live fearlessly and confidently.

Panic Versus Prayer

When a child has a scary experience, how do you react? Reprimand him, tell him not to be afraid? Get upset and afraid yourself? Injuries and accidents are a big part of a mother's life, starting when baby learns to crawl and starts falling down the stairs. We have some pretty hairy days in the course of trying to keep these little ones alive.

One morning Carmen came screaming into the house with her front tooth broken off. She had been skating and a naughty boy tripped her on the sidewalk. My immediate reaction was simple panic! I felt sick all over. But you know how we mothers are; we know we *have* to control ourselves for the child's sake, so we manage to do it somehow. I knew it was important to have prayer for her immediately, so I took her on my lap and asked Jesus to take away the pain and help her tooth not to die—what was left of it! In that short prayer, our panic disappeared. Carmen said she felt no pain, but now she was concerned about what she would look like. So we asked the Lord to take care of that too, and then called the dentist. The experience could have been a traumatic one, including the week she had to go to school with only half a tooth while waiting for a cap. The Lord even covered that; she breezed through it without self-consciousness.

I can't help but think what could happen in a situation like this if I had given in to my initial fears and allowed them to throw a child into hysteria. It's so important to turn to the Lord immediately in an emergency, so that He can begin working right away before we do something dumb under stress. When Mother and Dad get upset in a frightening situation, whether it's a thunderstorm or a broken arm, that's when a child begins to feel insecure. Christian parents have a wonderful advantage here, because they know the power of God and how to use that power in a desperate situation. They understand God's promises and have that factual basis for faith. When a Christian parent reassures and prays with a child, it's not a psychological gimmick or positive thinking. It's setting the power of God's promises into action; it's confidence based upon truth. But if we allow ourselves to be fearful people, we will infect our children with fear. Here again, our *example* of confidence and faith is indispensable for raising confident children.

Preventing Phobias

There's another thing to consider when a child has a frightening experience, and that's the danger of what psychologists call a fear psychosis—things like hydrophobia (fear of water), claustrophobia (fear of small inclosures). These usually begin with one severely frightening experience. Shirley, a young mother, was gripped with an obsessive fear of water. It was generalizing to even such routine things as bathing a child or running the tap. Psychiatrists couldn't get at the cause of her fear until her mother came to visit. She casually mentioned a time when Shirley had nearly drowned in a river at the age of 18 months, and the mystery was solved.

A Christian parent can use the authority God has given him in prayer and literally prevent such a fear from taking hold. Satan sometimes exploits a fearful event and uses it against a child. We can stop him from doing this if we'll use Matthew 18:18, and use it with intelligence. One translation of this is, "Whatsoever things you prevent on earth shall be prevented in heaven; whatsoever things you allow on earth shall be allowed in heaven." Sometimes we refer to this as "taking authority over Satan." But this promise is not limited *only* to the works of Satan. It simply says, "whatsoever," be they satanic things, psychological, or just day-to-day cause-and-effect dangers.

We were visiting relatives in Montana, and Carmen (yes, she again! At this time only a four-year-old) was playing in the yard. Suddenly a teenage girl came barging in the door, carrying our child. Carmen was bleeding terribly and screaming. The girl had rescued her from a German shepherd that had nearly killed her. Her head was chewed in several places; there were puncture wounds all over where his teeth had penetrated the skull. It happened so quickly we were stunned! Our daughter nearly killed right underneath our noses—one more bite could have been her temple or her throat but for the fast action of that fearless teen. (Was she a guardian angel in disguise?)

The first thing we did for Carmen was pray for her, asking the Lord to take away the pain and heal any damage that was done. Then we began disinfecting the wounds and getting her to the nearest doctor. But I could see the emotional shock had potential for doing even greater damage than the wounds. So that night we took the promise of Matthew 18:18 and prayed, "Lord, you've said that we have power in the name of Jesus to bind and to loose, to stop and to allow. And so, in the name of Jesus, we take authority over any emotional damage that could come from this. We prevent fear from setting into Carmen's life and we stand against any effort Satan might make to take advantage of her mind." All those prayers were answered, in even greater measure than we expected. She slept soundly—with a head full of holes!—and afterwards had no headaches or pain of any kind. From that day to this, she has never had a fear of dogs. In fact, it was Carmen who talked us into getting the cute puppy who grew into our enormous family pet—an oversized, gentle German shepherd!

If a child has already developed a fear, large or small, it isn't too late to deal with it. Psalm 34:4 shows us what to do: "I sought the Lord, and he heard me, and delivered me from all my fears." As Jerry was preaching one Sunday night, he asked people who needed release from fear to raise their hands so that others could pray for them. At home, Christi asked, "Mom, should I have raised my hand? Do spiders count?" I didn't even know she had a fear of spiders; I'd been too blind to see it. Every night we had been finding a different spider dangling from a corner in her room; naturally she imagined that eventually one would drop on her nose as she slept! We prayed for two things that night: deliverance from the fear of spiders *and no more spiders* in her room. That was the very last night we saw even the slightest trace of either!

Nightmares and Bad Dreams

When a child wakes up crying from a bad dream every night, it's obvious there's something wrong. Sometimes a reason for insecurity, like being away from home or having Mother away for a day, can give rise to fearful dreams. Or the fear of failure, brought on by embarrassing experiences, or demands too hard to reach. Sometimes *we* cause our children's bad dreams. We create insecurity and fear of failure by nagging and harsh, unloving insults. (You dumb kid! Can't you ever do anything right!?) We've put too much pressure on the child, or laid out too many threats of "what's going to happen to him" if he doesn't shape up.

Then, of course, a child sees things that frighten him in the course of a day—a dog fight, or an accident—and his subconscious may bring it up during sleep. I can still remember my childhood fear of logging trucks. As a four-year-old standing on the street corner in our little town, I suddenly saw a huge monster coming straight toward me! It was enormous and it made the loudest noise I'd ever heard! If I had a bad dream after that, there was usually a logging truck somewhere in it.

When bad dreams happen frequently and a child dreads going to bed because he's afraid of the dream he's going to have, a concerned mother wants to help. Naturally, we'll do away with the things we see are causing it; but we don't always know the cause, and children can't necessarily tell us. One night I was putting Carmen to bed and said, as I habitually do, "Is there anything special you'd like me to pray for tonight?" "Yes," she said, "I had a bad dream last night. Pray that I won't have one tonight." Just then a promise came to mind, "The peace of God, which passes all understanding, shall *keep* your hearts and minds through Christ Jesus" (Phil. 4:7). I began to claim that promise every night for each child, and it's proven absolutely true. Their hearts and their minds are simply their *emotions* and their *thoughts*; awake or asleep, their emotions and thoughts can be guarded by the peace of God. The Greek word that's translated "keep" means "to guard; protect; actually to post a sentry," as you would to guard a fortress at night and keep out intruders.

When we mothers minister the peace of God to our children, in the name of Jesus, that peace stands guard all night long; and their minds are free from disturbing influences, no matter what the source of those influences. If you look at the verses preceding and following Philippians 4:7, you'll see there's a pattern involved in having the peace of God on guard continually. It includes learning: (1) to refuse worry, and instead (2) letting your requests be made known to God in prayer, and (3) controlling what's put into the mind. A child's mind should be occupied not with negative thoughts, or with ugly, repulsive things, but with those things that are true, honest, just, pure, lovely, of good report, virtue, and praise. If you can teach a child to pray about his problems instead of worrying, and discipline the material his mind feeds on, then you can claim the promise. Bad dreams and their emotional after effects can be prevented and your child can have a restful night free from fear.

Just now, think with me about the items listed in Philippians 4:8. Do they describe the content of materials placed in your child's mind today? If not, why not? What TV program did he watch last night before bed? A good comedy is harmless, but a detective plot with a murder case would be a bad choice; don't be surprised if nightmares come along. Some of the medical programs with emergency operations or patients being told they have an incurable disease—that's pretty negative stuff on which to send a child to bed. He identifies too strongly with those fictitious characters, even if you do tell him they're only actors!

The television industry is starting to hear the cry of parents against violence; we need to keep up that protest. Television violence is not only objectionable because it begets more violence, but also because it begets fear in large supply. I discovered that for myself in just two weeks. In our first months of marriage, Jerry's job involved staying at home every night to take calls coming into a funeral home. We developed the habit of watching whatever was on television each evening. In that city there were only two channels to choose from, and both ran a steady monotonous diet of cops-and-robber stories and western movies. Very shortly, I noticed my thoughts running in negative directions, depressing and fearful. In two weeks' time it became unbearable; I dreamed every night about chasing a crook or being shot at by a cowboy! We learned that you do live with what you put into your mind. If two weeks of negative TV can turn a happy bride into a morbid, fearful creature, what does it do to our children?

Synthetic Fear

Much of what I just said about television and children's fears could also be said about certain kinds of comic books and movies. We'll talk about those more in the next chapter, but much of popular entertainment is nothing more than synthetic fear, successfully marketed and frantically purchased by the consumer. The thing that amazes me is why people pay money to be frightened, and to experience things like earthquakes, monsters, the Exorcist, and worse. I have a difficult time understanding parents who allow their children to attend horror movies and watch sick occult programs on TV.

I believe that everyday life in the real world brings enough frightening experiences to a child; but when these are multiplied by a diet of vicarious fright, the subconscious mind reacts as though it had all actually happened. Adrenalin is pumped into the bloodstream of a child watching a TV thriller just as though he were actually being chased by that monster. His memory writes down the fears he feels and files them away beside the fears he experiences in real life. Our subconscious minds do not distinguish between fantasy and reality. They simply record faithfully the vivid experiences we put into them.

Synthetic fear is not valuable nor desirable in a society where real fear is plenteous. The scriptural basis for that statement is Proverbs 4:23: "Keep thy heart with all diligence, for out of it are the issues of life." The heart is the seat of the emotions, the will, thoughts, and memory. It's to be guarded—diligently protected. We can't expect a child to do this for himself. And God does not will for your child to grow up with fears and phobias. He doesn't want him hung up with psychoses and anxiety. That's why He's given your child parents—you—to guard carefully what goes into his heart.

Permanent Security

Have you ever related this verse to your child and his feeling of security? "There is no fear in love; but perfect love casteth out fear; because fear hath torment. He that feareth is not made perfect in love" (1 John 4:18). Both loving and being loved are needed by every child. Training, proper guidance and prayer alone won't provide the *security* a child needs apart from an environment of love and acceptance in your home. He needs the unshakable security of *feeling* loved by his parents, with no thought of losing that love. Our love for a child must be unconditional, not given as a reward for good behavior; it should be a constant factor he can always rely on. In young children especially, the greatest fear of all seems to be simply that of losing the approval of a parent. They need from us that perfect love that casts out fear—that toal acceptance and consistent relationship. This prepares a child to know and love his heavenly Father, so that he can find an even greater trust, a permanent security. He needs not only the love of parents but, again, the *feeling* that he is completely and totally loved by God. When he loves God and knows that God loves him, he has the potential for permanent security.

Have Your Own Bible Study
Children's Fears

1. Factual basis for fearless living: Ps. 91.
2. Preventing or curing phobias: Matt. 18:18; Ps. 34:4.
3. Nightmares or bad dreams: Phil. 4:4-8.
4. Synthetic fear—we don't need it: Prov. 4:23; Phil. 4:8.

5. Permanent security: 1 John 4:18.
Other promises for protection: Prov. 1:33; Ps. 3:5,
6, 4:8, 34:7; Prov. 3:23, 26; Luke 10:19.
Promises for healing: James 5:14, 1 Pet. 2:24;
Ex. 23:25; Deut. 7:15.

Chapter 11

Your Child and His Mind

I hope my impassioned attacks on television in the last chapter stimulated you to think about your family policy regarding TV viewing. Do you have a policy? In the next few pages, we'll suggest some scriptural guidelines for establishing a policy for television. I really don't *hate* TV—it can be a blessing instead of a curse if we use it to teach the things we really want taught. But with all forms of entertainment—movies, books, TV, and music—we must always keep in mind our stewardship of our children's minds; and, remember, those minds are not sieves but receptacles. The material we place in those receptacles shapes and molds little lives—important lives with an eternal destiny!

Parents who lived through the era of the Beatles can never forget the damage done to an entire generation in the sixties. Even Christian teens were led into drugs, sex, revolution and Oriental religions. Many of these kids had been raised on excellent Bible teaching. The example of Mom and Dad may have been faultless, their encouragement and correction perfectly consistent; but when mothers doled out the money to buy Beatle records, they took into their homes a force so powerful in the receptive minds of kids that gullible children were led to tragedy by the Pied Pipers from London. When parents finally found out what the Strawberry Fields Forever were all about, it was too late. Unfortunately, the impact of concepts and ideas repeated over and over in countless songs is still alive in the minds of much of the generation who lived through it.

The revolution is gone now; the rock groups fragmented. Most of us are alert enough to recognize a current group which surfaces after the pattern of the Rolling Stones or Black Sabbath. But I was a pastor's wife in the sixties—one of those helping to pick up the pieces of those shattered young lives, and I'll never forget it. I habitually listen to our local teen radio stations and monitor the records our children buy. If another wave of evil takes over the pop music world, I intend to know it before it's taken my children in its wake!

By the way, do you know you can influence the music that's played on the stations your children listen to, without investing more than the time it takes to make a phone call? Several radio stations have lost their licenses to broadcast because they've played songs with objectionable language or sexual subject matter. The Federal Communications Commission will refuse to renew the license of a station which has too many complaints against it for these things. And their license comes up for renewal every year. So a few phone calls from parents can make a station manager *very* nervous! Just make the call brief, polite, and say that as a parent you're concerned that they played "I Want to Sleep With You" (or whatever song you heard—just be sure to name it and say when you caught it). Tell them you would appreciate their taking a responsible attitude toward the children they're touching, and you're aware the FCC has also expressed concern for this.

There are plenty of good popular groups on the scene who put out acceptable music for kids and who do not sing dirty songs. The kids know who they are; and if parents will bother to find out who they are and be aware of what's going on, there is no reason for any radio station *not* to be responsible. We *can control* the airwaves, and if we *will*, we can also gain control of television stations in the same way—by letting our wishes be known.

Now maybe that sounds impossible to you, to listen

to that awful loud music and find out what the words are. It's not at all impossible. We have a policy that the girls can buy records with their allowance money, but if the songs are dirty, or suggestive, or have swearing or occult references—or anything else objectionable —then out it goes and their money was wasted. We've never had to throw one out. I enjoy lying on Christi's bed with her and listening to her latest purchase. We talk about the song and the singers; it's one of the door openers to conversation about how she feels about things. If Carmen is listening to her radio out in the yard, I use it as a good excuse to combine sunbathing with motherhood and we listen and talk about the songs. This whole approach of sharing a child's interests in books, music, etc., has a pleasant side effect! Mom gets many chances to rest!

The Consistent Computer

Students of the human mind have discovered that the mind is like a giant computer: it never really forgets anything. Each item placed inside is neatly filed away, ready for future use. You've perhaps heard of Maxwell Maltz's famous book, *Psycho-Cybernetics*, which explains the power of the subconscious mind. Most of us realize that the conscious mind—the part of the brain we are most aware of—is really only a small part of the equipment God gave us. The subconscious mind compares in size and capacity something like the unseen part of an iceberg. When you observe an iceberg, you may feel you're looking at a pretty big chunk of ice, but an iceberg doesn't float on top of the water. From two-thirds to nine-tenths of it lies submerged, invisible to a casual observer. (Remember the Titanic?)

The subconscious mind of your child is like the submerged, invisible part of the iceberg. What's in the subconscious mind is what really matters, because it's basically out of what's stored there that we make decisions, come to conclusions, speak opinions and feel desires toward right or wrong. Everything that goes into the subconscious mind will eventually be used by the person who stored it there, whether he stored the material deliberately or carelessly. And furthermore, everything that goes into it must come through the five senses; the child stores what he reads, experiences, hears on the radio, sees on TV and at the movies. This becomes his basis for living. That's why I want to emphasize again the command of this verse, "Keep thy heart with all diligence, for out of it are the issues of life" (Prov. 4:23). That's the Bible's more succinct way of stating all that I've just written on this page!

Think on These Things

Many of our homes operate on a policy of expediency when it comes to what's placed in our children's minds. We do what's convenient, even when it works against our long-range goals for the children. Television is such a cheap baby-sitter. And shipping the kids off to a Saturday afternoon movie is an easy way to get Mom some hours for herself—especially during school vacations, when all the troops are underfoot whining, "We don't have anything to do!"

I was an avid moviegoer for a short period in my late teens. One day, after a quite ordinary, typical movie, the Lord laid this scripture heavily upon me, "Whatsoever things are true, whatsoever things are honest, whatsoever things are just, whatsoever things are pure, whatsoever things are lovely, whatsoever things are of good report; if there be any virtue, and if there be any praise, think on these things" (Phil. 4:8). I became alarmed, because that list did not exactly describe the thoughts that a movie generally brought into my head. In fact, people and events made up of truth, honesty, justice, purity, loveliness, virtue and praise—those are just not popular in Hollywood! They claim they can't make money on movies like that!

We avoided taking our girls to any movies, even good ones, until they were around ten. When they were preschoolers, we'd pass a drive-in and they'd say, "Mommy, why don't we ever go there?" The answer would go something like this: "We really don't have time; but, also, we don't like to see ugly things, and they show a lot of killing and witches and monsters—real *icky* things. We don't want to watch that or watch people doing wrong things with their bodies. We want you girls to have happy thoughts and good dreams. We wouldn't think of taking you to a place where you'd have to see gross things or get scared or sad."

That's not just the way I explain it to a child; it's exactly the way I feel. Finding a good movie is like digging through a garbage can to get a sandwich at the bottom.

Even Dr. Spock, author of *Baby and Child Care*, says some strong things about movies and the mind of a child. Thought by most parents to be a liberal, still he writes, "Movies are a risky business under the age of seven. You hear of a program, let's say an animated cartoon, that sounds like perfect entertainment for a small child. But when you get there, you find, three out of four times, that there is some episode in the story that scares the wits out of little children. You have to remember that a child of four and five doesn't distinguish clearly between make believe and real life. The only safe rule that I know is not to take a child of under seven to a movie. Don't even take an older child to the movies if he gets frightened easily." [1]

Dr. Spock also writes about television and sounds more like an old-time Bible preacher than a permissive liberal. "Children's fascination with television brings up several problems—the first is with the child who is so scared by the tales of violence that he can't go to sleep at night or has nightmares. Another problem is with the child who is glued to the set from the minute he comes in, in the afternoon, until he is forced to go to bed at night. He doesn't want to take time out for supper, for homework or even to say hello to his family. It's better for the parents and child to come to a definite understanding about which hours are for outdoors, for homework, for meals, and for programs, and then for everyone to stick to the bargain." [2]

Scripture Speaks

Here are verses I feel apply to setting guidelines for what we place in children's minds through movies, TV, books, and music:

Proverbs 15:13, "A merry heart makes a cheerful

countenance; but by sorrow of the heart the spirit is broken."

Proverbs 15:17, "A merry heart doeth good like a medicine, but a broken spirit drieth the bones."

Is happiness one of your goals for your child? Do you like to see him laugh and smile, sing and joke with you? So much of what a child sees on TV and movies can militate against a merry heart and a shining smile (cheerful countenance). So ask the question, Does this program fill a child's mind with happy, pleasant thoughts or does it encourage depression and sadness? The morbid, the horrible, the violent and frightening will soon add up to "sorrow of heart" and rob him of that natural childlike happiness.

Proverbs 24:1, "Be not envious against evil men, neither desire to be with them. For their heart studies destruction and their lips talk of mischief."

Proverbs 23:17, "Let not thine heart envy sinners; but be thou in the fear of the Lord all the day long."

Ask, What values are communicated to children by this program? What kinds of things are being made to look glamorous and exciting? What kinds of people are ridiculed? Does the villain have your sympathy because he is misunderstood and treated unfairly by the law? Are loose living playboys the heroes your boy will emulate and are girls taught to pattern themselves after women living with men and sleeping around? In some shows, the sinner's life is made to look appealing, while the life of an upright, stable man looks dull. How many homes are faithfully teaching that the way of the sinner is hard, that unhappiness goes along with a life of ungodliness, only to have that teaching undermined by stories that entice a child into envying the sinner.

Then there are the movies and programs which promote witchcraft and occult interests. And those which make lying and cheating acceptable. (Killing is wrong, but lying is all right. The cop who virtuously catches the evil robber turns around and seduces a woman or gets drunk—and this cop is the hero!)

Creative Alternatives

One of the sad effects of the TV generation is the stunting of creativity. Children who have great potential for creativity have their senses dulled by a steady diet of canned entertainment. Try turning off the TV for a week and see the change in their play. We used to have only a small portable I could simply hide when we wanted to encourage reading or creative recreation. Whenever I hid it I made sure there were plenty of unread library books on hand, interesting records, piano music to play, and construction paper for art projects. We've enjoyed reading books aloud together as a family. Some of these books I've heard more than once, and even loved them the second time around, especially Mrs. Piggle Wiggle! We've read *Charlotte's Web*, all the Henry Huggins books (those are *so* hilarious!), the children's fantasies of C. S. Lewis, *Chronicles of Narnia*, plus countless other Christian books. I've found that if I'm alert to guide them, our children prefer these activities almost any night to what's on television.

Let's take seriously our stewardship of the precious minds entrusted to us. Let's fill them with love and beauty, purity and wholeness, honesty and peace. Let's allow them to be all that God intended, unhindered by morbid fear or dull insensitivity.

Have Your Own Bible Study

Your child and his mind: Prov. 4:23; 15:13-17; 24:1; 23:17; 12:5 and 8; Phil. 4:8.

Chapter 12

Your Child and His Friends

To what extent should a mother control the friendships of her children? The popular notion is no control at all. Let a child choose whomever he wants to play with, or go steady with, or race cars with—or steal cars with! The most common cliché that comes up in conversations of mothers is, "After all, you can't choose their friends for them!"

Who said so, anyway? The Bible says nothing remotely resembling that theory, either directly or indirectly. When we set about to study the scriptures on this subject in a Touch of Beauty Bible study, we were amazed to find it had almost as much to say about friends and their influence as about heaven or hell! In this chapter, we'll include around fifty of the verses we read, but you can find probably a hundred more on this subject, if you read the Bible and check all the verses having to do with friends. As we first began reading, one young mother exclaimed, "I've been doing it all wrong! My daughter was smarter than I was! Here I've been encouraging her to be friends with everyone, good or bad, and she's been telling me she feels uncomfortable trying to hang around the rough kids at school."

Shirley was honest enough to take the Bible as a guide for motherhood, even at a point when it didn't agree with the opinions she'd already formed. The warnings in the Bible about wrong companions are based on the fact that those companions can lead a person into Satan's traps, and can lead my child—even a child from a Christian home—straight into hell. You see, a child's friendships are not simply a matter of temporary indulgence in drugs or sex. It's not the teenage trips that are so damaging, it's the destiny of those trips—the possibility that the end of them could be death and a Christless eternity for the child I love so much. My child's eternal destiny is far more important to me than his social acceptance, his popularity, his fun and thrills. It's even more important than his comfort and my convenience.

Proverbs 13:20 is clear in describing the cause-and-effect relationship: "He that walks with wise men shall be wise, but a companion of fools shall be destroyed." The fool is defined throughout Psalms and Proverbs in many ways, but basically he's a rebel in every possible sense. So if we allow our child to spend time with a rebel, we're placing him in danger of destruction.

Proverbs 22:24: "Make no friendship with an angry man and with a furious man thou shalt not go; lest thou learn his ways and get a snare to thy soul."

Proverbs 2:10-15: "When wisdom entereth into thine heart, and knowledge is pleasant unto thy soul; discretion shall preserve thee; understanding shall keep thee: to deliver thee from the way of the evil man, from the man that speaketh froward things; who leave the paths of uprightness, to walk in the ways of darkness; who rejoice to do evil, and delight in the frowardness [rebellion] of the wicked; whose ways are crooked; and they froward in their paths." That's a good verse to read with children, perhaps from a simple translation. It lists some of the characteristics of wrong friends. That chapter of Proverbs keeps talking like that and when we come to verse 16, it says, "To deliver thee from the strange woman, even from the stranger which flatters with her lips."

Here's a good warning and also a promise, if you happen to have one of those good-looking teenager boys that the girls are crazy about. If you want to keep him from dating the kind of girl who will destroy him, teach him the Word of God in such a way that God's wisdom actually enters his heart—becomes a part of him and is pleasant to him; he enjoys and loves the Word. In the Living Bible this passage reads, "Only wisdom from the Lord can save a man from the flattery of prostitutes; these girls have flouted the laws of God. Their houses lie along the road to death and Hell. The men who enter them are doomed. None of these men will ever be the same again." In these days of excessive sexual temptation, we need to make sure our sons are aware of both the warnings and promises of God. The same goes with daughters, of course. Boyfriends and girlfriends are certainly one of the strongest factors in this area of friendships. *Whatever* you have to do to keep your boy or girl from a dating relationship that's leading him down the road to hell—for *heaven's* sake, do it! Don't be intimidated by the happiness or unhappiness of the moment; consider your child's eternal destiny. Consider the plan that God has for his life. How many teens have messed up that plan hopelessly because of a lack of supervision in their dating life.

A good scripture to teach Christian children on this, of course, is 2 Corinthians 6:14: "Be not unequally yoked together with unbelievers; for what fellowship hath righteousness with unrighteousness? And what communion hath light with darkness? And what concord hath Christ with Belial? Or what part hath he that believeth with an infidel?"

Parents Refuse Responsibility

In previous pages, I referred to the stories in *Parents on Trial.* This subject of friendship played a major part in the answers given by the parents asked about their delinquent sons:

Bobby's mother had wept bitter tears over a boy who was killed in a robbery. Her answer to Wilkerson's question was, "I had a bad boy because he got in with the wrong crowd." She said she had laid down the right rules for him, but Bobby had had bad friends and they had led him astray. It was not her fault. Mother wanted no part of the blame. Hers was a good home, neat, comfortable, and containing everything a child could want. Next, the minister went to visit a Mr. Rogers. "Please tell me," he said, "honestly, simply, why did your son become a drug addict?" Mr. Rogers answered, "Reverend, I can tell you in two words—bad friends. They led him astray. *We* loved him. *We* took him to church. *We* gave him everything he needed. Sammy just ran with the wrong kids."

As he writes about this incident, Wilkerson says, "Mr. Rogers was right, as far as he went in his thinking. It was Sammy's friends who had led him astray. But why had Sammy run with the kind of teenagers who were a bad influence on his life? Home is where we learn to set standards and develop our value systems. Perhaps Sammy's parents were delinquent in not giving this kind of instruction or in failing to set the right kind of example. When Sammy began running with the wrong gang, what did his parents do about it? They simply scolded him; they did not offer him any alternatives. I have known many parents who have, often at great sacrifice, moved to a different neighborhood when they saw their children headed the wrong way. The Rogers family could have moved, but it was *convenient* for the parents to stay where they were. They paid dearly for this convenience." [3]

As Wilkerson's account goes on, he tells how he gained almost no insight from the parents. None of them could see that they had anything to do with the delinquency of their child! So Wilkerson went to the kids he worked with—converted junkies, addicts and prostitutes. He asked them what their parents could have done to prevent them from going wrong. Among other things, Tony said, "I read once, 'If you tell me who your friends are, I'll tell you what kind of person you are!' This is true. Parents should know a lot about the neighborhood they live in. If it's a bad neighborhood, they should either move out or keep an extra eye on the kids. It's pretty easy to fall in with the wrong bunch because there's so much temptation, most of it fun to a kid." Another young man named Lewis said the same thing about friends. "Parents should make sure their kids have the right friends, good friends, and teach them the right way to live." [4]

What impressed me was that even delinquent children expect their parents to do something about the friends they run with. How tragic when parents refuse that responsibility!

How Can We Recognize Wrong Friends?

In our Bible study with mothers, we read through a list of scriptures (listed at the end of this chapter) and asked four questions. As we found words or phrases in each verse to answer these questions, we listed them on our chart under the appropriate question. We asked:

1. What commands are there about a child's choice of friends?

2. What are the characteristics of wrong friends?

3. What are the dangers or results of spending time with wrong friends?

4. What are characteristics to look for in choosing right friends?

Some of the characteristics of wrong friends were put down in the verses I've already shared. Did you notice them? A really definitive list of characteristics is found in 2 Timothy 3:1-5, which ends its thought by saying, *"From such turn away"*!

"Remember this! There will be difficult times in the last days. For men will be selfish, greedy, boastful and conceited; they will be insulting, disobedient to their parents, ungrateful and irreligious; they will be unkind, merciless, slanderers, violent, and fierce; they will hate the good; they will be treacherous, reckless and swollen with pride; they will love pleasure rather than God—keep away from these men."

Some of the personality traits on that list also appear in this descriptive passage in Proverbs 1:

"If young toughs tell you, 'Come and join us—turn your back on them! We'll hide and rob and kill,' they say; 'good or bad, we'll treat them all alike! And the loot we'll get! All kinds of stuff! Come on, throw in your lot with us; we'll split with you in equal shares.' Don't do it, son! Stay far from men like that, for crime is their way of life, and murder is their specialty. These men trap themselves! They lay a booby trap for their own lives. Such is the fate of all who live by violence and murder. They will die a violent death" (Prov. 1:10-19).

That's a pretty timely description of today's neighborhood gangs and the shoplifting thrill seekers—or the tragic end of the SLA.

Here's a passage that seems to anticipate the rise of groups like the SLA or the Weathermen. Such youthful groups dedicated to violence are really nothing new on the scene; they're a fact of history. They didn't actually begin with the young Nihilists in pre-Communist Russia (early 1900's). They were around in ancient Israel and a well-known fact of life in surrounding nations.

"My son, fear thou the Lord, and the king: and meddle not with them that are given to change: for their calamity shall rise suddenly; and who knoweth the ruin of them both?" (Prov. 24:21, 22).

A few more verses about characteristics of wrong friends:

Proverbs 14:7, "Go from the presence of a foolish man, when thou perceivest not in him the lips of knowledge."

Proverbs 23:20, "Be not among winebibbers; among riotous eaters of flesh: for the drunkard and the glutton shall come to poverty."

We can safely conclude that the kind of children or teenagers who are not to be allowed as friends would be those who are lawless, rebellious, greedy, angry, violent, bitter, tough, sneaky, unstable and hateful. They're disrespectful to parents and teachers, living solely for pleasure and thrills, scornful of society and their country, foolish and unkind. They use obscene and profane language, are gluttons and drunkards, dissolute and undisciplined in their life-styles, reckless and proud of it.

If you note carefully, in each of these lists of wrong friends, there's an accompanying commandment. It did not say, "My son, get to know these fellows and spend time with them so you can win them to Christ." There are kids that my child can win to Christ, but they do not fit into that list of rebels. No, the Bible says, "My son, if young toughs invite you to spend time with them, *refuse*—turn your back on them." Don't even apologize for that; you have no obligation to them. There can be no honest friendship on a continuous basis between a child of God and a child of the devil. You can love these people and treat them kindly, but your obligation *is not companionship or intimate friendship.* All the people I minister love to and treat kindly are not my daily companions, or those I invite to meet me for lunch! The Bible makes a distinction between friendship and love. God loves the sinner but He certainly does not adopt the sinner's life-style so that He may show that love. God calls that sinner to repentance and when he comes to Him, cleans up his desires and attitudes and sinful nature. Then that sinner is ready to receive Christian friends.

Why Do We Cop Out?

Many pressures come to a mother who takes her responsibility in the friendship realm. You can really get into hot water with your kids! And maybe even with the neighbors! Neighborhood pressure in some areas is strong; you become most unpopular if you refuse to let certain children play at your house or in your yard. You're very aware their parents gossip about you over their coffee up and down the street! ("She seems to think her children are too good to play with ours! And claims to be a Christian, no less! What kind of Christian love is that, I ask you?")

I can still remember my mother calling us to come in whenever certain boys came into the yard or began to hang around us in the woods next door—even when we were three and four. We'd call back, "Why do we have to come in? It's not dinner time yet." And she'd say, "Don't ask. Just come." She never failed to do this, at any time of day or night those fellows should appear. And she was right; we didn't know what was wrong with them; but they all went the route of de-linquency eventually. Yes, she was unpopular with the mothers of those kids. Probably they did gossip. She felt it was a calculated risk worth taking.

We've repeated the same pattern with our children. I'm sure I have made enemies, been misunderstood and gossiped about. Looking back now at the children I didn't allow as friends when Carmen was five, the disapproval of those mothers seems a small price to have paid.

We have had a policy of not allowing the girls to stay overnight with girlfriends (unless we're travelling, of course) or have them overnight here. That includes slumber parties, which really makes me unpopular. "But, Mom, why can't I go? She's a nice girl. She'll think I don't like her." I say, "Tell her your mean mother won't let you go to slumber parties. That's just the way it is." I'd rather take the blame and have parents or their kids feel insulted by me than put that on the girls. Their disapproval can't hurt me nearly as much as the results of copping out can hurt me. (I would never condemn another mother, incidentally, for having slumber parties or allowing them; this is just a policy for our family, set in a fast-growing city and a faster-growing church.)

When children argue, pout, or rebel at your decisions about friends, stand firm. The Bible doesn't guarantee that your child will enjoy the discipline you bring to him. But it does guarantee that wise guidance will deliver his soul from hell and produce an adult who will bring you joy.

Family, Fun and Friends

Two verses that give positive guidance toward right friendships are Psalm 1:1 and Proverbs 27:17. In the first Psalm we see that right friendships are an integral part of happiness: "Blessed [happy] is the man that walketh not in the counsel of the ungodly, nor standeth in the way of sinners, nor sitteth in the seat of the scornful." "Standing in the way of sinners" is a good phrase. It pictures a person "just hanging around"—with the wrong companions. Another verse about the tie between happiness and right friends is in Proverbs 27:9: "Oil and perfume rejoice the heart; so doth the sweetness of a man's friend that cometh of hearty counsel" (RSV). And in the same chapter, there's an observation that can be taken as advice in choosing a good friend: "Iron sharpeneth iron; so a man sharpeneth the countenance of his friend" (Prov. 27:17, RSV). Right friends will bring out the best in your child; the two together will sharpen each other.

I see this principle at work regularly, when Christi is with friends from her youth group and Carmen hangs out at "the Barn" (our youth building—it really is a barn, too). Whether they're playing pool, or lying on the bed listening to records, the effect of being together is warmth, happiness and growth in character.

In the book I referred to earlier, *Parents on Trial*, David Wilkerson follows his observations about wrong friends with some advice to parents: "A youngster must be taught and encouraged to choose wholesome companions. It is difficult to find a case of narcotics addiction among young people that was not induced by association with the wrong kind of companions. Youngsters should be encouraged to bring friends home for supervised activities and they should be guided to the kinds of places where they will meet the sort of friends they would be proud to bring home with them. These friends can be found at church, in scouting, youth camps, and the like. They are not likely to be found in billiard parlors or on street corners." [5]

I especially like to give big parties for the children now that the Lord has blessed us with a big house. But even before, at birthday times, if Carmen would invite thirty friends, that gave me a chance to know them and be aware of which would be good to encourage her to have over often. We like to have church friends over for Sunday dinner and the afternoon. And one of the reasons for moving to the big house was because it had such potential for recreation—a pool, play yard, space for ping-pong and pool, foosball, etc. There are always things for friends to do together, and there's nothing more pleasing to my ears than the sounds of that!

Have Your Own Bible Study

Your child and his friends

Use the scriptures below to find God's answers
to these questions:

1. What commands are there about a child's choice of friends?

2. What are the characteristics of wrong friends?
3. What are the dangers or result of spending time with wrong friends?
4. What are characteristics to look for in choosing right friends?
    Ps. 1:1; Prov. 1:10-19; 2:10-20; 13:20; 22:24; 23: 19; 24:21, 22; 2 Cor. 6:14; 2 Tim. 3:1-5.

Chapter 13

Honesty

Isn't it a traumatic experience for you when your child tells a lie? Or is yours so perfect he's never done that? (Don't we wish!) When that angelic little two-year-old looks straight at you with innocent eyes and jam on his face and says, "Sally did it, Mom," the mess he just made doesn't bother you half as much as the realization that he's just a little sinner after all! He knows how to be naughty, hateful and dishonest without even being taught! So we have to start early explaining the difference between fact and fancy, truth and lies. We have to teach why lying is wrong, and we have to train a child not to do it by seeing to it that the punishment for lying is always enforced.

Paul wrote to the Ephesians, "Wherefore putting away lying, speak every man truth with his neighbor." An interesting note in the margin of my Bible says this, "It was a common thing for heathen teachers to declare that a lie is better than the truth when it is profitable and less hurtful. Having been brought up in such a loose system of morality, these converts needed this admonition." Well, those heathen teachers were into the same philosophy that is prevalent today—situation ethics and relative morality.

To the Colossian Christians, Paul said, "Lie not one to another, seeing that ye have put off the old man with his deeds" (Col. 3:9). Christians lying to each other? Really? Those Christians, who gave their lives for Jesus, who witnessed so powerfully? Yes, even they had to be reminded to tell the truth, and even to tell it to each other! I'll never forget my initial shock at finding out there are still some Christians who have this habit.

A teenage girl accepted Christ at the church and her life was drastically transformed. She won several other kids to the Lord, and there was no doubt that she really did encounter Jesus. She had been in the church about seven or eight months when she was caught in a bold-faced lie. Looking into it further, we found she habitually told lies whenever it was to her advantage. It was a left-over from her old way of life—part of this old man and his deeds Paul talked about. It was so much a part of her that she herself hardly knew when she was lying and when she was telling the truth. Her mind had been conditioned so that it no longer distinguished between truth and fiction. At first I thought this must be a phony, someone who had just pretended to be a Christian. But that wasn't true. She was sincere in her commitment. She was now at exactly the spot some of the new Christians in Colossae were and had to have it explained to her: "Now that you're serving Christ, you have to stop lying. That's part of your old life-style. It was to be put off, as you would take off an old coat and throw it away."

She was the product of a pagan society, a home that had never taken time to train honesty, never developed her mind to distinguish between truth and untruth; and she's not at all different from thousands of teens growing up in America today. It used to be different here, because the country was based upon Christian values and a consensus of opinion that right was right and wrong was wrong. Just about everyone agreed that lying was wrong, stealing and cheating were wrong—period. Now we have a society that is questioning whether they are wrong. Such things as absolutes and honesty are becoming rare, much as it would be in a pagan culture where there was no knowledge of God.

Some of our friends were in a section of Africa as missionaries where idol worship prevailed. The culture had such a different basis for thinking that no concept of truth even existed. No one told the truth about anything. They would simply say whatever was convenient or whatever they would like the truth to be. As they lived among these people, the missionaries found you could never depend upon anything they said—it was more likely to be a lie than the truth. The people had no conscience qualms at all. Lying was a way of life and the culture was built on that base! It was a chaotic culture, too, with no security for anyone, much hatred and misery. But that's the end result of ignoring God and His standards of right and wrong. There are masses of people right here in our land who are doing just that—making up their own rules. Our children will be affected by that kind of thinking if we don't make a serious effort to counteract it. Even the comedy shows on television often teach that small lies are okay; only big ones involving money are wrong.

Honesty in the Family

Today's mothers have to work for honesty in their family. It won't happen accidentally, because we're living in a society where fewer and fewer people practice it. Women cheat at the supermarket, married couples fudge on their income tax returns, men steal supplies from the office they work in, and far from hiding it all, they brag about it to their friends.

I talked with the wife of a young man who made a good salary but had become such a habitual thief that a day never went by when he didn't bring something home from work. He worked in a place where many nice things were shipped out and, by doctoring up the shipping orders, he could take all kinds of tools and equipment home without being discovered. He had a garage full of things he would never use but would probably sell to friends. He was becoming a miserable person to live with, but didn't seem to feel guilty about his stealing and lying. There are lots of men like this— no trace of honesty left in their lives; and then you add to this the epidemic of shoplifting by women and teenagers, and it's quite obvious that integrity is breaking down in the society we live in. As Christian families, we must guard ourselves from slipping into even the smallest forms of deceit and robbery.

Many television programs teach by inference that

lying is okay if you can get away with it. This element in so many of the seemingly harmless comedies is difficult to nail down. Sometimes a whole story will be built around a lie someone told and got away with, and it's a hilarious program that you really enjoy. We need to make a strong effort to clearly teach honesty and offset this. We train honesty by *example, explanation, experiences, encouragement* and *correction*, just as we do every other character trait.

What is your example of honesty teaching your child? When he overhears your conversations on the telephone, is he hearing a different story about what happened last night than the things he actually *saw* happening? If you're stopped on the highway by a policeman, does he see you reply with truth? If you're diligent in your verbal teaching about truthfulness, then your children will notice even more each small part of your example.

One day I took our small daughter into a coffee shop for a Coke. As we were driving home, she was very disturbed about something. Finally, she said, "Mommy, you stole that Coke from the lady!" "What?" I exclaimed! "You never paid her!" I had been so absorbed with our conversation, I had walked out without paying. Have you ever done that? Isn't it embarrassing? We had to drive back right away and pay our 30¢, and I reassured her that Mommy wasn't really a thief, just absent-minded sometimes. That incident made me aware of how closely our children watch us, and how quickly we can undo our most lofty words.

When a child is old enough to talk, to understand us, then is when we begin instruction about truthfulness. We explain what a lie is, and why it is wrong. Stories about children who told a lie and then felt very bad about it provide a good starting point for a discussion like this.

In explaining honesty, let us be sure to show that telling a lie is not wrong merely because you'll get caught, or because there will be punishment, or even because your conscience will bother you. True, these things are result of lying, but the reason it's wrong is because *God said it's wrong*. Even if Mommy didn't think lying was wrong, it would still be sin, because *God* said it was.

We teach this concept when we use the Scriptures as the ultimate authority with a child. As we take time to teach verses about honesty, we place in his mind the understanding of absolute standards of right and wrong, standards that do not change with the crowd you're with or the philosophies of politicians. You introduce the child to a Person who will still be his authority, even after you're gone.

Teach the Bible

Proverbs 12:22: "Lying lips are an abomination to the Lord: but they that deal truly are his delight."

"Abomination" is a big word for a child, but it never fails to catch their attention. "What's 'abom . . . abom . . . abonimation,' Mom?" they'll be sure to ask. I usually answer, "It's something that makes you sick to your stomach—something you just can't stand."— And one will say, "I can't stand broccoli!" And you can explain, "Stevie, that's the way God feels when someone tells a lie; He hates lies. But when you tell the truth, even when it's hard, the Lord is very happy with you. You're His delight."

Another good verse for children is Proverbs 19:5: "A false witness shall not be unpunished, and he that speaketh lies shall not escape."

You can explain two things in this verse. Number one, if someone lies in our family, Mommy *has* to punish them. But, number two, even if Mother or Daddy didn't punish you for lying, you would still be punished in some other way, because lying has its own punishment built right in. I deliberately do not say, as some do, "God will punish you!" It's too easy for us parents to present God as a policeman, someone sitting in heaven with a big club in his hand, watching to see if you're going to step out of line so he can "get ya." God does punish sin, that's true; but generally He doesn't have to initiate any action against the sinner, because sin has its own inherent penalties. And Satan uses the sins of the sinner to increase his misery.

My husband tells the funny story of his childhood when they sang a song in Sunday school that said, "There's an eye watching you." He pictured God as a great big eye in the sky, keeping him under surveillance all the time. If he got in a fight with the bully at school, that big eye would be watching and he'd say "get him!" If he argued with someone over a ball game, the big eye would say, "He slipped again! Get him!" Until this concept was remedied, the poor boy felt God was mad at him all the time. How could he love a God like that? So watch your teaching of the Scriptures so that you don't over-balance the loving Father you want your children to know with too much fear.

Two other good verses for study with children are: Psalm 119:29: "Remove from me the way of lying: and grant me thy law graciously"; and Psalm 119:30: "I have chosen the way of truth: thy judgments have I laid before me."

Isn't that a beautiful confession? "I have *chosen* the way of truth." This is a good verse to use with a child who has told a lie and needs to be dealt with about it. He needs to get it out in the open as soon as possible, take his punishment, and then find forgiveness, both from his parents and from the Lord. When the spanking is over, sit down with him and say, "You've had your punishment, and I know you won't tell any more lies. We're going to forget all about it, but wouldn't you like to ask *God* to forgive you? And to help you not do it any more?" One of God's great men prayed that way once. He said, "Remove from me the way of lying. . . . I have chosen the way of truth." If you can help a child to pray that way, and assure him of God's forgiveness, the whole experience can be one that will strengthen him rather than tear him down.

One night I was putting my children to bed when our seven-year-old asked, "Mommy, what is cheating?" "Well," I said, "cheating is when you take answers off someone else's paper at school. They do the work and you steal the answer. Cheating is a combination of lying and stealing. It's lying because you make the teacher think you did the work to get those answers. That's not fair, because you were supposed to do it yourself. The Bible says that the Lord hates cheating, and that's because it hurts you and it hurts other people." She began to cry and said, "Well, Mommy, I did that, but I didn't know it was cheating till now. Nancy said that she would do half the problems on our math and give me the answers, if I would do the other half and give her the answers. Then we'd both have our assignment before recess. So we did that yesterday and today, but I didn't know you weren't supposed to." The poor girl was really upset about it after hearing that God hates cheating. She prayed a sincere prayer of repentance and asked Him to forgive her. I felt very bad, because I realized she really didn't understand what cheating was. I had said that it was sin to lie, steal and cheat, but I had never explained the meaning of the word cheating. That's just one example of the way we parents sometimes take things for granted. I'm just thankful the Word of God corrected that problem before it became a habit, because once a child develops the habit of cheating in school, all kinds of dishonesty enter in and his conscience gets hardened.

We need to be explicit in our teaching. We need to apply the scripture we read children to their lives at school and in the neighborhood, and do it in specific ways that they can understand. Here are some verses you can use with your child.

Have Your Own Bible Study

Honesty

1. Lying: Prov. 12:22; 19:5; 26:24, 25; Col. 3:9; Eph. 4:25; Rev. 21:8; Ps. 55:21; 101:7; 119:29; 120:2.
2. Stealing: Lev. 19:11; Eph. 4:28.
3. Cheating: Deut. 25:13; Prov. 11:1; Lev. 19:13; Jer. 22:13; 2 Cor. 8:21; 1 Thess. 4:12; 1 Pet. 2:12.

Chapter 14

Children's Quarrels: Causes and Cures

Children's quarrels—what do *you* do about them? A lot of American mothers have a simple answer: Do nothing! They rationalize that it's healthy exercise for the kids, releases tensions and teaches them to stand up for their rights. After all, "Kids will be kids," they say. "All brothers and sisters fight. It's part of growing up."

If you're like me, you like a peaceful house and detest listening to squabbling youngsters. But we live in a society which increasingly seems to feel a peaceful home or a peaceful marriage is something too abnormal to be acceptable. Marriage counselors are encouraging husbands and wives to have a "good clean fight" to clear the air. Child psychologists advise that it's a healthy outlet for kids to have it out with each other. They should be left alone while they slug it out in the bedroom. Sensitivity groups are formed to give sinners a place to express their sin, their hatreds against each other, their vile thoughts and mucky emotions. All this is made to sound moral and wholesome by titles like honesty, facing yourself, self-realization and "telling it like it is."

The Bible doesn't agree with the philosophy that fighting is a good thing. In fact, it seems to say that God wants me to have a family life of peace. At least, that's what I conclude from reading Psalm 133:1: "Behold, how good and how pleasant it is for brethren to dwell together in unity." Consider that verse in connection with your family. I like to insert the word "sisters" because we have girls: "Behold, how good and how pleasant it is for sisters to dwell in unity." So often I experience those exact feelings when my grownup sister and I are together. The fellowship we enjoy is beautiful and never fails to make a happier, stronger woman of me. We've enjoyed hiking along the beach, exploring forest trails, listening to beautiful music, studying the Bible and praying together.

Julie is one of my closest friends, besides being my little sister. I hope my two daughters enjoy this kind of love for each other as adults. What if Julie and I had been allowed to fight with each other? What if we had grown up in a home where quarreling and strife were the norm? We've never had to overcome bitterness, resentment, jealousy or hatred, as do children who've been allowed to hurt and cut with angry words. As adults, we've shared the same home on several different occasions—sometimes for a whole summer and sometimes in very crowded conditions. According to the great thinkers, we're abnormal because we've never quarreled. It's not because either of us is perfect. Julie and I both happen to be strongly individualistic, with decidedly different opinions and tastes. But we both love Jesus, and the unity we have in Him frees us to love each other. We value the fact that in a home where strife was not accepted, we were taught to love each other.

But a common, and sad, story goes like this: "A brother offended is harder to be won than a strong city, and their contentions are like the bars of a castle." "Their contentions" are their arguments, their quarrels. These build a wall that is very difficult to tear down between two brothers—a wall of suspicion, defensiveness, resentment and bitterness. As a mother, why let these walls build up and ruin a potentially wonderful lifelong relationship?

Why not instead use this as a pattern for life in your home: "Let all bitterness, and wrath, and anger, and clamor, and evil speaking, be put away from you, with all malice: and be ye kind one to another, tenderhearted, forgiving one another" (Eph. 4:31, 32). In Colossians there's a similar passage, ending, "Forbearing one another, and forgiving one another, if any man have a quarrel against any: even as Christ forgave you, so also do ye" (Col. 3:8-13). The Bible doesn't go along with the psychology of rude honesty and does not view quarreling as healthy. It warns against angry arguments, name calling and tensions between people. In nearly every book of the New Testament, strife is condemned as an unfitting activity for Christians. Romans 12 asks us to live peaceably with all men, as much as it lies in us (v. 18).

Here is God's opinion of strife: "Now the works of the flesh are manifest, which are these: adultery, fornication, uncleanness, lasciviousness, idolatry, witchcraft, hatred, variance, emulations, wrath, *strife*, seditions, heresies, envyings, murders, drunkenness ... they which do such things shall not inherit the kingdom of God" (Gal. 5:19-21). If strife is counted among those despicable sins by the Lord, then I certainly don't want my children growing up feeling it's normal! When Paul wrote to the young pastor Timothy, he said, "But foolish and unlearned questions avoid, knowing that they do gender strifes. But the servant of the Lord must not strive [or argue], but be gentle unto all men, apt to teach, patient."

The Old Testament has even more to say about strife, and none of it the least bit tolerant. Proverbs mentions it in at least twenty-five different verses and, indirectly, in dozens more. In fact, the person who starts a fight is listed among seven things the Lord hates. It's named as a mark of a truly wicked man in Proverbs 6:12: "A naughty person, a wicked man, walketh with a froward mouth. He winketh with his eyes, he speaketh with his feet, he teacheth with his fingers; frowardness is in his heart, he deviseth mischief continually; he sows discord." So if you have a child who's always picking a fight, he's headed for real trouble unless you can change his habits. It may be something more serious than "just a stage" he's going through.

Each year, in my Junior High School classes, I seemed to have at least one of these kids. Wherever he was, there was discord. It didn't matter what group you put him with, an argument would begin. Starting a fight was a way of getting attention from kids and teachers, or an expression of hatred and rebellion, or an excuse to lash out at others for the hostility he felt inside toward himself. It is pathetic to see kids like this grow worse and worse in their relationships, graduating from quarreling to stealing cars and joining gangs. The principal, counselor, and teachers often worked many hours to try to salvage this kid, to no avail. His parents had neglected to train him in getting along with people. This starts, not in the classroom, but in the home, where he lives with brothers and sisters in peace. That's why we have a rule against arguing in our home, just like we have a rule against jumping on the couch or coloring on the walls. Part of my job as a mother is to teach my children how to love one another, in spite of personality differences.

One more verse that's good to remember when you're cooking a steak dinner and the kids are screaming at each other is Proverbs 17:1: "Better is a dry morsel and quietness therewith, than an house full of sacrifices with strife." A "house full of sacrifices" refers to meals of the finest meat. How often do we welcome a husband to a good meal, only to have it ruined by quarreling children! The Bible can show us how to have a peaceful home where brothers and sisters dwell together in unity.

Let's see what practical suggestions we can find in the Word of God about the way to do this. Before we understand the cures of quarreling, we need to set down some of the causes.

Quarreling: The Bible Lists Causes

It's pretty obvious that brothers and sisters will fight because of sibling rivalry, jealousy, a desire to attract attention, or, just to get their own way. Sometimes parents unintentionally provoke children to resent one another—comparing one brother unfavorably with another, or giving more praise and attention to one than the other. The Bible warns against this in Ephesians 6:4, "Ye fathers, provoke not your children to wrath." In Colossians 3:21, "Provoke not your children to anger, lest they be discouraged." This includes all the varieties of parent-caused strife, like strident yelling and harping at them, haranguing and arguing, rather than expecting obedience. It also includes our mistakes of playing one child against another, such as, "Why can't you get good grades like your brother?" Or, "Notice how neat and nice Marcia keeps her room, and she's much littler than you, too!" If you talk like this, it's not surprising if big sister soon begins to slip in little digs at Marcia, designed to bring her ego down to size—things like, "I think your coloring is sloppy." Or, "You act like a baby!" Then Marcia, if she's normal, will get upset and retaliate. When Mommy comes in to break up a fight, she decides that big sister was the culprit who started it. But perhaps we need to ask ourselves if we've been careless in seeding resentment in big sister. Even aside from that, kids also get jealous and selfish without our help. (They're human like us!)

Laying aside the parent-caused kind of strife, let's consider some verses from Proverbs which define other causes. Proverbs 15:18, "The wrathful man stirs up strife: But he that is slow to anger appeases strife." Proverbs 29:22, "An angry man stirs up strife." Proverbs 28:25, "He that is of a proud heart stirs up strife." Proverbs 26:20, "Where no wood is, there the fire goes out: so where there is no talebearer the strife ceases." If you have a tattletale in the neighborhood, I'm sure you agree with that one! Proverbs 26:21, "As coals are to burning coals, and wood to fire; so is a contentious man [an argumentative one] to kindle strife." Proverbs 22:10, "Cast out the scorner [or the criticizer] and contention shall go out: yes, strife and reproach shall cease." Proverbs 16:28, "A froward man sows strife and a whisperer separates chief friends." A "froward man," by the way, is one who turns away from righteousness, the rebel who knows right but does wrong anyway. And, then, there's that old ego, which causes a lot of arguments, even children's arguments. Proverbs 13:10, "Only by pride comes contention [quarreling], but with the well-advised is wisdom."

A very familiar verse, "A soft answer turneth away wrath, but grievous words stir up anger" (Prov. 15:1), is a concise definition of the way any argument starts, whether between five-year-olds or fifty-year-olds. Someone says some grievous words, an insult, criticism, or a brother orders his little sister around in a superior manner—and the fight is on!

Meddling is another source of strife named in the Bible. Proverbs 20:3, "It is an honor for a man to cease from strife: but every fool will be meddling." This is common in children's quarrels. Johnny tries to show Tim the correct way to tie a bow, and little Tim beats him off. He wants to do it himself! The little sister insists upon playing games along with big brother and his friends; she meddles, strife transpires. We can cut down quarreling if we teach children how not to be busy bodies and meddlers.

Often strife takes place just because kids are kids and not altogether smart yet. Proverbs 18:6, "A fool's lips enter into contention, and his mouth calls for strokes." Contention is arguing, and a fool just constantly gets himself into arguments. When you remember the verse that says, "Foolishness is bound up in the heart of a child," you can understand one reason kids fight. They're not naturally wise about handling their problems, but, with proper training, *they can learn.*

Proverbs 10:12, "Hatred stirs up strifes: but love covers all sins." If hatred develops between children of the same family, there's bound to be strife. We must help our children learn to love each other, forgive and never get into the habit of building up resentments that can turn into hatred. If hatred is causing strife between two children, it's because the parents have allowed that hatred to develop.

In this hurried survey of scripture, these are the causes listed for strife: anger, pride (ego out of control), a scorner (or criticizer), a talebearer (tattletale), contentious person (or quarrelsome child), meddling, grievous words, a froward person.

We've also noted parent-caused strife (or provoking children to anger): comparing children, unbalanced attention or praise to one child, yelling and nagging.

Cures for Quarreling

When a doctor treats a patient, he's interested in

destroying the cause of illness, not merely the symptoms. It's possible that in dealing with children, we can frustrate ourselves by treating the symptom (the quarrel) instead of the cause (anger, hatred, parent provocation or criticism). So, taking the various causes in turn, let's see what anti-virus medicines the Bible has to prescribe.

We can prevent most arguments in our homes if we prevent criticism. We have a rule against it in our house and, although enforcing it is sometimes tough, it *is* easier than breaking up fights. So many sisters and brothers grow up with a habit of criticizing one another. Kids will do this; no one has to teach them. But it always leads to quarreling. That's why the Bible says, "Cast out the scorner and strife will cease" (Prov. 22:10). If you notice a child is continually picking at his brother's faults, then try this verse to get rid of strife. Take the fault-finder out of the room. Let him play by himself until he learns not to criticize. His brother will never be perfect, so if he wants the fun of playing with someone, he will have to learn to accept people as they are.

Learning not to criticize is a valuable lesson in the right use of our mouths, one we must give our children. Proverbs 18:7 warns: "A fool's mouth is his destruction, and his lips are the snare of his soul." To let a child go on with his mouth out of control is really the cruelest thing you can do for him. That mouth will destroy him and his soul!

Some mothers find a bad mouth can be improved by washing it out with soap. Whatever you do, don't allow a child to stand and argue with you, or to pick arguments with others. If you can make him control his mouth, he can learn to discipline himself, and that's an important part of growing up.

Anger is another of the causes of fighting and this, again, is an area in which a child needs to learn self-control. There will always be those situations that make us angry, but fighting never solves them. Anger can be turned away, the Bible says, by soft words. Teach a child about this and how to speak kindly to a person who is angry, or even to speak kindly when he himself is angry. Your example will influence this. If he sees you yell and shout when you're angry with him, he will learn that's the proper way to behave. But if you say, in a quiet controlled voice, "Johnny, I'm very angry with you, because you have been doing what I asked you not to. Now you go sit in the corner by yourself until you can mind." Then, he's learning a different way of handling anger. He's seeing the meaning of a soft answer that turns away wrath.

Jealousy and Selfishness

When you see a pattern of arguing based on jealousy or rivalry, take a look at yourself. Does it have a basis in your partiality to one child? Usually when this happens, it's accidental. We just happen to give Cindy a little more attention than Lisa because Cindy has started school and brings home lots of interesting papers. Lisa feels neglected then and gets jealous and resentful.

However, if selfishness is the usual cause of quarrels between Lisa and Cindy, you'd take a different approach. Here's a good suggestion from the Bible if the problem is just two kids wanting their own way about a tricycle: Proverbs 18:18, "The lot causes contentions to cease, and parteth between the mighty." Here's how it reads in a newer version: "The lot puts an end to disputes and decides between powerful contenders." Drawing lots was similar to tossing coins, but not exactly the same. I've tried tossing a coin, or drawing straws to settle children's disputes, but then found they argued about who could choose first. So I looked into the meaning of this term, "drawing lots," and found they would put the people's names on pieces of paper, then draw one out of a bowl—just like you draw names for Christmas. If Jimmy's name is drawn, he gets to ride the trike first today. That ends the argument and everyone is satisfied. This is more sensible than letting them use brute force, which is never fair because the biggest bully will always win that fight!

Distract and Divert

Another handy verse for a mother who hears a fight developing is this: "The beginning of strife is as when one lets out water: therefore leave off contention, before it be meddled with." That's Proverbs 17:14, and it warns us to stop the quarrel before it really gets going. You can, for example, divert attention to a new activity by sending the fighters on an errand, outside to play. Or maybe it's time for an afternoon snack.

Proverbs 21:14 says, "A gift in secret pacifies anger." A secret gift is that little nice something you suddenly bring in the room; it distracts attention from the anger, whether it's cookies or a new idea for playing. Proverbs 12:20 states, "To the counsellors of peace is joy." Learning to be adept in counselling peace to children is one of the joys of motherhood. Don't you just feel a lot better about yourself when your children are playing happily together?

One of the verses I like to stress in teaching my children, at the times when no one is fighting, is "Blessed are the peacemakers" (Matt. 5:9). We talk about how the word "blessed" means "happy." When two children fight over something, the child who feels happy is not the one who gets his way. The child who makes peace is the one who feels happy. Then after we've taught about this, and a quarrel gets started, we can ask, "Who wants to be the peacemaker?" Preschoolers, especially, respond beautifully to this.

Another cause of strife you run into, as soon as your toddler learns to talk, is the one Proverbs calls talebearing—tattling. This is a ticklish one because we all know there are times when a child should tattle—when there's an emergency, danger, or a serious problem. We have to teach them how to discriminate between these times and the trivialities. When our children were around three and four, we taught them about tattling and other childish faults by means of what I called "Cynthia stories." Cynthia and her little sister Susie were the subject of all kinds of tales we'd invent according to what needed emphasis. One of their neighbor boys was very lonely. No one wanted to play with him because he was a tattletale. His presence in the story was a gentle reminder against tattling.

Answer Not a Fool!

Now there's one last thing I'd like to share—it's

advice for us mothers: Do not argue with your children; and don't let them argue with you. Proverbs 29:9, "If a wise man has an argument witha fool, the fool only rages and laughs, and there is no quiet." Furthermore, "It is an honor for a man to cease from strife" (Prov. 20:3). "Answer not a fool according to his folly, lest thou be like unto him" (26:4). If you argue with a contentious child, you're as foolish as he is, and, he loses respect for you. A child will never learn obedience from a parent who argues with him. Let your home be dominated by an atmosphere not of strife but of peace and love and pleasant words.

Have Your Own Bible Study

Children's quarrels—causes and cures

1. God's will for peaceful family life: Ps. 133:1, 2; Prov. 18:19; Eph. 4:31, 32; Col. 3:8-13; Rom. 12:18.
2. What God thinks about strife: Gal. 5:18-21 (strife among the "works of the flesh"); Prov. 6:12 (mark of a wicked man); Prov. 17:1 (in the home).
3. Causes of quarreling: Eph. 6:4; Col. 3:21; Prov. 29:22; 15:18; 28:25; 26:20, 21; 22:10; 16:28; 13:10; 15:1; 20:3; 18:6; 10:12.
4. Cures for quarreling: Prov. 22:10; 18:7; 15:1; 18:18; 17:14; 21:14; 12:20; Matt. 5:9; Prov. 29:9; 20:3; 26:4.

Chapter 15

Your Child and School

Sooner or later, it seems, every mother encounters school problems; like a ten-year-old who's convinced he hates school and wishes it were spring vacation from August to June; or a second-grader who feels strangely sick in the morning and amazingly healthy as soon as the bus has gone. Then also there are the learning problems: Cindy crying because she can't get her math; Jim hating to read aloud; and the adolescent girl who wants constant excuses from gym. Social adjustments are a big part of school, too, and children will come home upset because of personality clashes. One day my daughter went off to school with a new hairdo. I thought Carmen looked pretty with her long red hair lightly curled. But *she* came home crying because another girl had teased her all day, calling her "curly head"! Some of these social problems seem small to us as we wrestle with high finance at the grocery store, but to a child these are not small.

A five-year-old may be afraid of a large dog on the way to kindergarten, a tall boy, the principal, the janitor or even going to recess! When I was little I was afraid to walk past a certain house every morning, because I had heard those people had a fox in their backyard!

It's all these little challenges and a child's learning to meet them that produces maturity. He *can learn* to handle them if we give him the right attitudes, training and confidence. If you've been an overprotective mother for the first five years of a child's life, it will end when he starts school. Because there's no way you can protect him from all these little (but big to him!) problems that will now confront him. You're forced to train him how to relate to people, how to handle hard situations, and how to live.

I read through the book of Proverbs, noting verses that apply to a child at school so that I could teach them to my children. I want to share those verses with you and ways you can guide your child in successfully meeting the challenges of school. I'm using the word "challenges" rather than the word "problems." That's because there's a negative, fearful connotation to the word "problem," while there's a positive, optimistic connotation to the word "challenge." Life is full of challenges; that's what makes it exciting!

One of the main differences between a happy and an unhappy woman is that one sees her life as one of continuous challenge, the other sees it as one of continuous problems. The same approach holds true with children. If they're upset about something at school and your reaction is to get upset too—lash out at the teacher, cry over your mistreated, suffering baby— he'll quickly learn to think in terms of problems. But if you think in terms of challenges, then your reaction to the same situation will go something like this: "How can I guide him in handling this? What valuable things can he learn from the experience? What does the Bible say about it? How does this event fit into the business of growing up and learning to live with people?"

Here are a couple of verses that tell you how to react when a child has a problem: The first one tells you what to *say* to him. Isaiah 35:4, "*Say* to them that are of a fearful heart, Be strong, fear not!" Right before it is a description of what you're to *do* for that child, "*Strengthen* ye the weak hands and *confirm* the feeble knees." Joshua 1:9 is a verse to prepare them with the right attitude toward challenges at school: "Be strong and of good courage: be not afraid, neither be thou dismayed: for the Lord thy God is with thee withersoever thou goest." That concept and that confidence will put starch into even your first-grader. When he really believes it and is taught to live it, he won't become an overdependent "mama's boy." He'll be a success in school and in life.

I'd like to discuss the child who just doesn't want to go to school at all. However, I can speak only from positive experience because, so far, our children think school is a picnic. The worst punishment we could invent would be to make them stay home. But since they're normal in other ways, there will probably come a day when one feels mysteriously sick and stays in bed too late to catch the bus. It's then I'll need to remember similar days in my own childhood, the frightening test a teacher had promised, or the embarrassment connected with just walking down the hall as a high school freshman. I can remember times when it seemed so much more secure to stay home in a cozy house with a cozy mother than to go out in the rain and face those classmates and teachers! It's the desire to do the comfortable thing, even when you know the more difficult thing is best for you. There's something frightening out there, and you're torn between facing it and escaping it. So the six-year-old has butterflies in his stomach on the first day of school, and the high school freshman does too.

One day I was on our local college campus during registration. There was a large room filled with forms, tables, and secretaries where lines of confused-looking young people stood. No one had to tell me those were the college freshmen. I couldn't help but wonder how many would drop college before they even finished registering! A few months ago, they were the cocky, lighthearted seniors. Now they're facing all over again a new adjustment, unfamiliar territory—a confidence-shaking, demanding challenge. A large percentage of them won't make the adjustment. They'll turn and run from it because of mothers who gave in to escape techniques like a sick headache. Some of them had overprotective parents, fearful parents, who didn't guide them into self-confidence.

Courage and Confidence

If you're the parent of a two-year-old, start now

to teach him confidence and courage, even a certain amount of independence. Leave him at home with a baby-sitter occasionally—it will do him as much good as it does you! Take him to Sunday school and don't rush to take him out of class when he cries. Don't let that one-year-old bluff you out of the church nursery, either! One hour away from Mommy won't damage him, even if he cries the whole hour. As soon as he finds you're not hearing his tantrum, he'll find better ways to entertain himself, like playing with other toddlers, which is the best way to begin learning to relate to people. It'll save you many headaches later.

A good thing about Sunday school is that it begins at an early age to teach the confidence-building concepts of Scripture. Some of the typical memory verses from toddlers classes are, "Be not afraid, the Lord is thy helper"; "I will trust the Lord"; "The Lord is with thee to keep thee in all thy ways"; "I will never leave thee nor forsake thee"; "Call upon me and I will answer thee, saith the Lord." By the time a child goes to school, he has a wealth of scripture stored in his mind and, with it, a deep security and confidence. He's conscious of the presence of Jesus with him wherever he goes; and he knows he can call on the Lord for help in a problem. That makes it a whole lot easier to leave Mommy and get on that school bus! And if a child has learned to know Jesus personally, has gained a habit of praying about his problems and seeing them taken care of, then there are fewer chances he'll be unhappy in school. He'll have the resources to meet new situations.

School Phobia

How should a parent react to children who invent excuses to stay home from school? I was amused to read Mrs. Piggle Wiggle's suggestion for the problem. (Have you heard of Mrs. Piggle Wiggle or read any of the books about her? If not, you really ought to get some from the library, and settle down for a few hours of uncontrollable laughter. They're children's books. Kids start bringing them home from school when they get to be eight or nine. Mrs. Piggle Wiggle is this neat little lady who loves children and knows how to cure their ailments. The parents in her town call her for advice on curing tattletales, interrupters, never-want-to-go-to-bedders, quarrelers and children who won't clean up their rooms.)

One story we read aloud with our family was about Allen, the slow-eater-tiny-bite-taker. It did wonders for the slow-eater-tiny-bite-taker in our house!

The book has a story called "The Never-want-to-go-to-schooler." It starts with a scene in the Jones boys' bedroom. It's morning and Jan and Jody are arguing about a toolbox. Then, "There was the sound of footsteps on the stairs. Jody threw himself back in bed and began to groan. Mrs. Jones walked over to the bunk, reached up and felt Jody's forehead. She said, 'You haven't a speck of temperature, Jody, so stop playing possum and get up.' Jody groaned loudly and agonizingly. He said, 'My stummick hurts awful. It feels like I swallowed ten knives!' Mrs. Jones looked worried. She said, 'Where does it hurt, dear?' Something like that goes on every day, with Jody convincing his parents he's sick while the children know he's not. Finally, Mrs. Piggle Wiggle has a magic cure called ignorance tonic. After two days of taking the medicine, Jody decides he *wants* to go to school. Because the ignorance tonic did exactly what its name implies— it brought on total ignorance. Jody became as though he'd never learned anything. He couldn't remember how to talk, count past three, he hammered nails with his pliers instead of the hammer, and used a spoon when he should have used a fork. He suddenly became terribly ignorant and all the children called him stupid. After two days, Jody realized that school had something to offer him after all, and maybe it wouldn't be much fun to go through life without an education.

Ignorance Is Danger

That part of the story is true, even though we don't have such a thing as "Ignorance Tonic" to prove it. If we did, we could, like the magic Mrs. Piggle Wiggle, convince a child of the value of an education. But first, the parents need to be convinced that going to school is important and that a lack of education *is* a serious handicap. If you're convinced of those two things, you'll not be letting Jimmy stay home very often, and you'll not tolerate a bad attitude toward school or reading or learning of any kind. Christian parents have a basis for this in Scripture. The Bible places a high premium on learning, knowledge and education. It warns about the dangers of ignorance, and has promises about the increase of a child's intelligence. Some of these attitudes are listed in Scripture. Proverbs 1:7 "Fools despise wisdom and instruction." Does that sound like a kid who hates school? Isn't that what he's hating, in the end—wisdom and instruction? Another verse is Proverbs 13:8, "Poverty and shame shall be to him that refuseth instruction." If that's true, then a child who doesn't go to school can expect to be poor and miserable. You may have to support him in your old age! Proverbs 15:32 says, "He that refuseth instruction despises his own soul." Those are just a few of dozens of comments from the Bible about right and wrong attitudes toward learning. It's important that mothers have a godly attitude toward learning and transmit it to their children.

Educators know plenty about the mysterious illness called "school phobia." It's a common thing in child development. In this illness, there are often real physical symptoms—vomiting, stomachache, headaches, dizziness—but when the doctor examines Susie, he finds nothing to account for them. If he's your family pediatrician, he'll probably give you his diagnosis as "school phobia," and tell you to treat it like this—return Susie to school, immediately. The longer she stays home, the harder it will be to return and the worse the disease will become. If she has a relapse at school, there's a nurse who can treat her as well as you could and bring her home, if needed. Secondly, without making a big issue of it, find out if there are problems at school she's upset about. Talk to the teacher. Maybe there's a bully on the playground who pushes her off the swings, or she's not understanding the assignments and is afraid to ask teacher for help. Smoothing out these little pressures can make it less frightening to go to school, and you can avoid the worse problem of "hate school-itis." Face it, you just don't learn much when you hate school. You're there in body but not in spirit, always wishing you were somewhere else, and paying only half-hearted attention to the lessons taught. You do lack-a-daisical work and fall behind and things get harder and harder.

A good attitude toward school is an indispensable quality. To go through school without learning anything is to grow up without an education. In our country, that's almost a more serious handicap than a physical handicap, like blindness or paralysis.

Here's more of what the Bible says about the dangers of ignorance and lack of education: Proverbs 14:15 says the uninformed, ignorant man is gullible and vulnerable to exploitation: "The simple believeth every word: but the prudent man looks well to his going." Proverbs 13:18, "Poverty and shame shall be to him that refuseth instruction." Proverbs 14:18, "The simple inherit folly: but the prudent are crowned with knowledge." Proverbs 15:21, "Folly is joy to him that is destitute of wisdom, but a man of understanding walketh uprightly." Proverbs 19:2, "That the soul be without knowledge, it is not good."

When those concepts are a part of your thinking, Mother, then it's likely you'll have an unbreakable rule in your household—school attendance every day, Monday through Friday. The taxes you pay for schools and teachers will not give your child a quality education unless *you* get him there. You might as well get the most out of your tax dollar and get the best-educated children that can be had. So many rich opportunities for development of skills and learning and social growth are there, right in your school district, that you'll do yourself a favor if you train your child to have a healthy love for learning; a desire to learn new things—like soccer, saxophone, gymnastics and drama. Desire for learning, curiosity, alert minds and understanding heads—those are positive character traits encouraged by the Bible.

Godly Attitudes

Now perhaps you've heard the line of thinking that

says, "Education doesn't matter. It's not book learning that counts, but spiritual learning. It's not man's wisdom we need, only God's wisdom." That's only partly true. The fear of the Lord *is* the beginning of wisdom. True wisdom and knowledge rest upon God and His laws in every field of study.

However, in the view of the Bible, it's not necessarily spiritual to be uneducated or ignorant. The goal of a Christian home is *balanced* growth in four areas: spiritual, physical, social and mental growth, as we saw earlier in the life of Jesus.

Jesus was not handicapped by a lack of education. Jesus' parents held the views of the Old Testament on education, and those views considered it very important; even the poorest Jewish family sent its children to school regularly. Here are some of the things they believed from the Old Testament: "Bow down thine ear, and hear the words of the wise, and apply thine heart unto my knowledge. For it is a pleasant thing if thou keep them within thee: they shall be fitted in thy lips" (Prov. 22:17, 18). "He that getteth wisdom loveth his own soul: he that keepeth understanding shall find good" (19:8). "Hear counsel, and receive instruction, that thou may be wise in the latter end" (19:20). "There is gold and a multitude of rubies: but the lips of knowledge are a precious jewel" (20:15). "The heart of the wise teaches his mouth, and adds learning to his lips" (16:23). "Through desire a man, having separated himself, seeks and intermeddles with all wisdom" (18:1). "The heart of the prudent getteth knowledge: and the ear of the wise seeketh knowledge" (18:15).

That last verse states just the attitude I want for my children—a heart that reaches out to gather knowledge and an ear that eagerly listens to teaching; a healthy curiosity to know and comprehend; to understand the world and things going on around him: a value system that places more importance upon wisdom and learning than upon material possessions. Like in Proverbs 16:16, "How much better is it to get wisdom than gold! And to get understanding rather to be chosen than silver."

Learning Problems

When it comes to learning problems with a child —such as a slow learner, late bloomer, or a child with a reading block of some kind—it's great to be a Christian mother. We don't have to passively accept the problem; we can use the power of prayer and the Word of God to bring healing and permanent recovery.

If your child has learning problems, you can remember the promise in 1 Timothy that says, "God has not given us a spirit of fear, but of power, love and a *sound mind.*" I know of examples where God has demonstrated that promise to parents in a definite, miraculous healing of what appeared to be a low IQ. There's so much in the Bible about soundness of mind that we have to conclude the Lord wants to make our children whole mentally, just as much as He wants them whole emotionally and spiritually. In chapter 5, I referred to Psalm 119:130 and Proverbs 1:4, which declare the power of the Word to give "understanding to the simple" and "subtilty to the simple"—intelligence to the stupid! This is not a superstition; it's a demonstrable truth, and many parents have seen mental release in slow children by simply reading the Scripture aloud with them daily. One friend had a son who had a mysterious block to reading during the first six grades. By adolescence, he was hopelessly behind in all subjects because of this inability to read. It was a painful experience for both Myra and Johnny when Myra instituted a new decree. Johnny had to read aloud one chapter of Proverbs or Psalms to his mother each morning before breakfast—it took nearly a half hour! But his grades went in one report period from D's to C's, then up to B's. The mysterious reading block was snapped! John went on to become an honor student in high school and college.

Social Problems

Many children are successful intellectually but can't make the social adjustments. Their confidence is so shaken by one or two kids who don't like them, or tease them that they withdraw into a world of their own or become so insecure they tag along with any group demands. If a child is having social problems at school, you'll usually know about it, at least by the time his report card comes home. Probably somewhere on it there's a section labeled "Personal Development" or "Social Habits," and under it items like—plays well with others, is courteous, uses self-control, follows school rules, etc. That's an important part of the report, and if something negative is indicated, call the teacher and get more information on the problem. She may have a suggestion you'd value.

The Bible has some tremendous promises about identity and confidence. Psalm 119:23 and 24 records David's attitude when he was under social pressure. "Princes also did sit and speak against me: but thy servant did meditate in thy statutes. Thy testimonies also are my delight and my counsellors." Isn't that interesting? When attacked he meditated on the Word of God, and his confidence held firm. When a child is raised in an atmosphere of the teaching of the Scriptures, he knows who he is, he develops a strong identity and can handle the social threats. (See also Psalm 119:42, 51 and 52.)

Other verses talk about your child and social development: "My son, forget not my law: but let thine heart keep my commandments: let not mercy and truth forsake thee: bind them about thy neck: write them upon the table of thine heart: so shalt thou find favor and good understanding in the sight of God and man." That's in Proverbs, the third chapter. It's talking about the Word of God and its effect on a child. It connects a knowledge of the Scripture with two important consequences—favor with God and favor with man. Remember the growth of Jesus as a child? He grew in favor with God and with man, just as this Old Testament passage described. There was a parallel of spiritual growth and social growth. That's what God wants for your child, not some kind of spiritual mystic who's known at school as a weirdo! Keep alert to your child's social needs and social adjustment. Use biblical approaches to helping when he has a problem.

You Control Education

If we Christian parents will just be the salt of the earth in the schools of our neighborhoods, we can control what goes on. Salt gives flavor, acts as a preservative—a controlling factor against decay and corruption. Jesus told us to be the salt of the earth, but many of us have carefully bottled ourselves in the salt shaker —we've lost our savour!

It was Christian parents in this country who first came up with the idea of education. They built the first schools and hired the first teachers. And it's Christian parents today who have the strongest motivation for taking an interest in school. Knowing the influence it has on a child and knowing our responsibility before God, we have a stake in who teaches our children and what they teach. So, pay attention to what's going on. Listen to the stories Johnny tells about recess and gym class. Get a picture of what his classroom is like and what his teacher is like.

We've made it a practice to pray about the teacher who would teach our children each year. Beginning when Carmen started first grade, we prayed something like this: "Lord, we know you care about Carmen and the people who teach her. Work it out so that she will have a good teacher, someone who will not harm her in any way or discourage her from serving you, but someone who is either a Christian or a God-fearing person." Believe me, the results of those prayers have consistently delighted us!

"A wise teacher makes learning a joy: a rebellious teacher spouts foolishness" (Prov. 16:2, Living Bible). On that basis, pray for wise teachers for your children; and *do* something about it if your school is plagued with rebellious teachers spouting foolishness. The people of Berkeley, California, did not, and they suffered a decade of violence at the hands of radical professors leading students into riots. An interesting book about that and the events that made history on the Berkeley campus is *Teachers of Destruction* by Widener.

Also, you'd enjoy "Holy Hubert's" book, *Bless Your*

Dirty Heart. Hubert Lindsay was a well-known campus preacher at University of California and that's one of his trademark phrases—"Bless your dirty heart! Jesus loves you." His book is an account of a miraculous life and ministry among campus radicals led into revolution by professors salaried by their blindfolded parents. May the Lord give us the sense to be wiser than that in our city!

Here's another verse about teachers: Proverbs 17:21 "A wise man is known by his common sense, and a *pleasant teacher* is the best" (Living Bible). A pleasant teacher sounds to me like one who loves her students and enjoys her work. So that's another quality we want to seek out in hiring educators for our children.

"Stop listening to teaching that contradicts what you know is right" (Prov. 19:27, Living Bible). And you might also say, "Stop making your children listen to teaching that contradicts what you know is right!" There are ways of doing that! You do pay for your child's education and you have a right to say what is taught. Your influence in your school can make it a force for good on your child.

Reputation Trap

"Even a child is known by his doings, whether his work be pure, and whether it be right" (Prov. 20:11). That's talking about the reputation a child develops. Once he enters school, it's amazing how quickly he is labeled with a reputation. Have you ever thought about the fact that your child has a reputation? How do the children he spends each day with view him? What reputation does he have with teachers, with the bus driver and the principal?

Here's another translation of that same verse that may help our thinking: "It is by his deeds that a lad makes himself known if his conduct is pure and right." So a reputation is established not by some mysterious coincidence, but it's established by the actual things a child does. If he's rude to others, pushes and shoves, grabs the ball and the swing, he'll quickly be labeled with a negative reputation. If he mouths off to the teacher, and gives her dirty looks, he becomes known as a smart aleck, by both students and teachers. It's not attitudes or thoughts that determine a reputation; it's concrete actions. And that comes painfully home to us, doesn't it?

We had an incident several years ago that was painful to me. The teacher sent home a note saying our first-grader had hurt the feelings of another little girl in her class. She had teased her and made fun of her because she thought she dressed funny. I was the typical shocked mother: "I can't believe my perfect child would do a thing like that! After all, she's the preacher's daughter! And in a church where half the sermons are about loving and accepting people different from yourself!" Just reading the teacher's note, my face grew red! Now it wasn't an *attitude* that got my child in trouble, and it wasn't the teacher's prejudice against her. It was my daughter's unkind *actions*, revealing an attitude I hadn't even known was there—probably an attitude I had instilled in my efforts to send her off looking clean and well dressed every morning. So we had some careful discussions to get at the source of those attitudes. Our daughter shed many six-year-old tears when she realized how she'd hurt the other girl. She also shed tears when the punishment was doled out—a face-to-face apology to Susie, a spanking, and having her bike taken away for a week. That was hard for us all, but I'm so glad that teacher wrote me a note and let us correct the situation before it carried on into a pattern of behavior.

So often parents are in the dark until it's too late. That miserable experience taught my daughter to be considerate and kind, and did it before she had established the wrong reputation. And since then, at the first of every school year, I make it a point to meet the teachers and tell them I want to help in any way possible. We always say, "Please let us know right away if you have any difficulty with Christi or Carmen. Feel free to phone us any time. We like to get rid of problems before they grow into big ones!" Teachers appreciate that, and they remember it. When I was teaching, the parents who said things like that were the ones whose children I noticed. It was wonderful to know you'd have cooperation from the home when the majority of parents ignored your notes and requests for a conference. One man shouted and swore at me because his son came home with failing grades. The same father had ignored my warnings that his son would fail if he didn't get help from home.

There is a point when it's too late to change a child's reputation. The only thing left to do is move him to a new school so he can build a new one, among peers and teachers who won't hold him to the old name. If you do that, make sure it's done with prayer and careful preparation, both of the child and his new teacher. But don't let him endure the curse of a bad reputation. Until he's grown, you *are* responsible for that. You can control it because you can control his behavior. That kind of responsible motherhood is possible only when you have help; Jesus Christ must first be master of your life. When He is, there's no school problem too big to challenge His wisdom.

Have Your Own Bible Study

Your child and school

What does the Bible say:

1. About the dangers of ignorance (or "hating school"): Prov. 1:7; 13:8, 18; 14:15, 18; 15:21; 19:2.
2. About the values of education, learning and knowledge: Prov. 20:15; 16:16, 23; 22:17, 18; 19:8, 20.
3. About right and wrong attitudes toward school: Prov. 15:32; 18:1, 15; 22:17, 18.
4. About a child with a confidence problem: Isa. 35:4; Josh. 1:9 Jer. 33:3.
5. About learning difficulties and increasing intelligence: 1 Tim. 1:7; Prov. 1:4; Ps. 119:130.
6. About social adjustment: Luke 2:52—respected by peer group; Ps. 119:23, 24, 42—identity; Ps. 119:51, 52—independent confidence; Prov. 3:4—favor with man—respect of peers.
7. About a child's reputation: Prov. 20:11.
8. About teachers: Prov. 16:2; 17:21; 19:27.

Chapter 16

Affection and Acceptance

One thing Americans unanimously agree on is that parents should love their children. In view of that, it intrigues me that we hear so many people declare they never felt loved by their parents. We meet teen-agers on drugs who feel unloved, troubled ten-year-olds with ulcers, and college kids seeking to fill the void with sex. Over and over they say, "I never felt my parents loved me." And yet, if you were to ask the majority of those kids' parents, they'd declare honest-ly, "I gave him love. I really have loved my children."

Why is it that kids don't *feel* loved by parents who honestly do love them? And how important is that *feeling?* Which really matters in the end, the feelings or the facts? This hit home to me one evening as we sat in a couples' Bible study. My husband asked each person to describe the home in which he was raised. One of the questions was, "How would you rate that home in terms of the affection you felt there? On a scale of one to ten, with ten being an extremely affectionate home and one being a totally cold atmos-phere, where would you place yours?"

Now it happened that I knew each person in the room and almost all their parents. They were well-ad-justed adults from mostly Christian homes, and I would have guessed all of them to place their homes at be-tween five and ten on such a scale. But would you believe, every single one described his home as about a two or three in terms of affection? They said things like this, "I knew intellectually that my parents loved me, but I really can't say they expressed it verbally."

Or, "It was assumed we all loved each other, but, as far as affection was concerned, there was not much." One gal said, "Mom and Dad were very affectionate to each other, but they rarely hugged or kissed any of us kids." Another put it, "My parents found it hard to show their feelings. They seemed to be embarrassed about demonstrating affection." And still another said, "We had tremendous security and good discipline. We knew our parents wanted our best, but for them to come right out and say, 'I love you, Honey,' that just wasn't done."

As I listened to that discussion, I couldn't help but relate it to myself. I wondered if *my* children felt loved, because, apparently that feeling was missing in these otherwise conscientious homes. So I became curious to see if the Bible had any guidance for me.

In a Bible study, we went through the scriptures on the subject of love. There are three Greek words in the Bible translated love:

Agape—love of the spirit which takes place as God loves through us.

Eros—physical love experienced by the body.

Phileo—emotional love experienced by the soul, brotherly love.

Phileo love is the thing good friends experience. "I enjoy you, I like you."

Affection and Agape

Agape, divine love, is something we commit ourselves to do. It has the characteristics of being unconditional, unselfish and concerned with the good of the beloved. See 1 Corinthians 13. We see it lived out in the life of Jesus—loving with no ulterior motives, with no intention of demanding something in return. In explaining how *agape* love is action, not feelings, I made a list of the things it is not, things we often call love or confuse with love. For example, compassion, sympathy, empathy, pity and attraction—all emotions we feel at different times for people. Compassion says, "I feel sorry for you." But compassion is not necessarily *agape* love. God's love does more than feel sorry; it acts. Sympathy and empathy say, "I understand how you feel," or "I feel with you," but they don't always do anything helpful with the feelings. The word affection was on our list too as being a word *not* synonymous with *agape* love, even though we often use the words love and affection interchangeably. Affection is the verbal or physical demonstration of warm and tender feelings toward someone. Hopefully, it goes beyond the feelings of the moment and sincerely communicates a real love. But it is possible to feel affection or even show affection for a moment to someone you dislike in the everyday working relationship.

All these feelings I've mentioned are good. I'm not trying to say they have no value. I am pointing out, however, that they are not to be confused with *agape* love, that unselfish, unconditional acceptance we are to have for our children—the kind of love that holds steady through our emotional ups and downs, the kind of love which is not, in its essence, an emotion but a pre-determined pattern of behavior seeking the highest good of the child.

While *agape* and affection are two distinct qualities, both are to play an important part in a Christian's life. Romans 12:10 says, "Be kindly *affectioned* one to another with brotherly love; in honor preferring one another." Isn't that a good verse? Christians *are* to be affectionate people. The Greek term translated brotherly love is the word *phileo*, the emotional kind of love. We're to have that and *agape* too, especially in our homes.

For a Christian mother, the beautiful thing is that affection communicates much more than it ever could without Christ because we have the capacity to love children with *genuine agape love*. When we express affection, we are really saying more than the transient feelings of the moment. In no way is there a chance for our affection to be a mere show or a hypocritical thing. When Jesus is in your life, Mother, you have both *agape* and *phileo* love for your child, and you can express it every day!

Is Affection in the Bible?

An interesting study to pursue is to go through the

New Testament from Acts to Jude and make notes about the expression of affection in the early church. Jot down the passages encouraging Christians to be affectionate, and those using the Greek word *phileo* for love. Note the ways in which the early disciples expressed affection; for example, greeting one another with a holy kiss, or Paul hugging all the Ephesian elders as they hung on his neck weeping (Acts 20:36 and 37).

Ephesians 6:4 is addressed to parents: "And ye fathers, provoke not your children to wrath; but bring them up in the nurture and admonition of the Lord." Here the word nurture implies affection. It calls to mind a warm atmosphere of tender love. It's interesting that Paul would remind *fathers* to provide an atmosphere of nurture along with their godly teachings. A father is to be not just the firm, authority figure but also a man of tender love, a man who's not afraid to put his arms around his children. Mothers are told to do the same thing in Titus 2:4. They're given a job description from God's viewpoint and told to be learning to love their husbands and love their children. The Greek word translated love here is not *agape* but *phileo* —the affectionate term, conveying emotions, companionship, friendship. In other parts of the Scripture, we're told to love our children with *agape* love, but here the specific emphasis is affection.

Proverbs 4:1-4 is a scripture that sets a goal for me every day, starting as I send my children to school and extending to that bedtime kiss at night. The writer is talking to children about their parents and says, "Hear, ye children, the instruction of a father, and attend to know understanding. For I give you good doctrine, forsake ye not my law. For I was my father's son, tender and only beloved in the sight of my mother. He taught me also, and said unto me, let thine heart retain my words. Keep my commandments and live." Did you pick up the emotion in that verse? "I was my father's son, tender and beloved in the sight of my mother." That mother did a good job! Love was in her eyes, her touch and her words. She was able to leave that one overwhelming memory in the mind of a grown son that caused him to forever revere the teachings of his parents. No matter what ups and downs of living he passed through, there was the sustaining power of warm, reassuring, love.

Many grown children remember other emotions when they think of their mothers. They remember a nagging voice, an angry frown, a woman who never could be satisfied with them no matter how hard they tried. They think of the unappeasable tyrant, the gravel-voiced housekeeper who shouted, "Get your feet off the furniture! Pick up those shoes! You naughty brat! Wait till your father gets home!"

Isn't it easy, in our dutiful, conscientious correction, to forget about affection? Correction is needed; but affection is *just* as needed. One without the other will produce a mechanical, heartless child who could easily grow up with deep-seated problems.

What If I Don't Feel?

Unaffectionate people often rationalize that they don't want to be phony, and they are not going to express what they don't really feel. The tragedy there is that if they would begin to express affection, they would also begin to feel it. Just try it yourself. Give someone a few words of encouragement, or a gentle hug, and you'll find you *receive* something—a feeling stronger than anything you had for that person before! Our emotions are inevitably tied to our words and actions. They respond to what we say and what we do for others.

Actions trigger emotions—that's an important thing to remember! I first learned it, in a negative way, in a junior high school classroom. In my first months of teaching, I learned the hard way about discipline. In a class of forty kids, I was the naïve, intimidated little schoolmarm, being much smaller than the boys and looking nearly as young.

One night I was complaining about the smart-mouthed kid named Billy. My husband said, "I'll tell you what to do with him. Give him a mighty slap in the face the next time he mouths off." That sounded like good advice. So I went to school the next day prepared to do it. I waited until Billy said something loud and defiant; then I calmly walked to his desk, and without a bit of emotion, slapped him as hard as I could. The bully began to cry and look for a way to hide under his desk. The silence in that classroom was marvelous! But the thing I was not prepared for was the effect of that slap on *me*! In minutes, I went from feeling no anger to a state of what felt nearly like rage. I felt such anger I was afraid of what I might do next!

At home, I pondered my reaction. I slapped Billy, he cried, and I got angry! How strange! Gradually, I realized that our actions produce emotions in us—either negative or positive emotions.

If you want to feel more love towards a person, do something loving. If you want to feel more affection for your children today, start giving out the affection. Your feelings will follow along just fine. Take your little girl in your lap, cuddle her and say, "I love you, honey"; or grab your overactive four-year-old and give him a big bear hug. Tell him how much you love "Mama's boy." Maybe he will ignore you and run off to investigate another closet, but he needs it anyway. And *you* need it. Because the more you do that, the more honest feelings of affection there will be to carry you through those times you feel like giving him away! The more you've reassured him of your love and acceptance, the better it will balance out those times you have to spank and scold, *especially* if you have that overactive four-year-old tearing your closets apart! That kid will give you less opportunities to hug and kiss, but he needs it just as much as the cuddly one who never gets into trouble.

With each child, there may be a different way to express affection, but each one needs it—even the teenager who's too old to hold on your lap! He needs to find it in his home through quick, "casual" one-armed hugs, warm smiles and lots of verbalized acceptance.

Emotions Are OK

Children often behave not on the basis of what they know but what they feel. Our emotions are powerful. They control much of our behavior, even when we try not to let them. God built us with emotions; He didn't want mechanical robots. Healthy emotion and the expression of it is a valid part of balanced living. So then how much of the healthy emotions do you produce in your children, Mother? Is most of your relationship to them creating anger and resentment and very little of it creating warmth and tenderness? God designed your child to need affection—the outward demonstration of love. He planned for you to meet that need and to do it in such a way that your child will not suffer insecurity or feelings or worthlessness. These will offset the unhealthy emotions he'll experience from the world.

My pursuit of biblical direction on this matter of love and affection led me to decide several things. I decided *never* to become so out of the habit of saying, "I love you," that it was a struggle to get the words out. I decided to keep holding a girl on my lap as long as she'd let me—even if she was almost as big as Mom! And I decided to keep up the practice of kissing them good-bye every morning as they go out the door to school (which I originally started to reassure frightened first-graders), and to keep up my bedtime prayers and kisses always.

We really can't give too much affection, can we, in a world where even children feel anonymous? Affection is simply the expression of the love we have for our children—let's express it daily.

Have Your Own Bible Study

Affection and Acceptance: 1 Cor. 13; Rom. 12:10; Acts 20:36, 37; Eph. 6:4; Prov. 4:1-4; Titus 2:4.

Books Quoted as Source Material in
How to Raise Good Kids

Baby and Child Care by Benjamin Spock, M.D., © 1968, Simon & Schuster.

The Christian Family by Larry Christenson, © 1970, Bethany Fellowship, Inc.

Dare to Discipline by Dr. James Dobson, © 1970, Tyndale House, Publishers.

Mrs. Piggle Wiggle by Betty MacDonald, © 1957, J. B. Lippencott Company.

Parents on Trial by David Wilkerson, © 1967, Hawthorne Books.